PENSACOLA FLAVOR

A Culinary History with Recipes

DUEL CHRISTIAN

AMERICAN PALATE

Published by American Palate
A division of The History Press
An imprint of Arcadia Publishing
Charleston, SC
www.historypress.com

First published 2025

Manufactured in the United States

ISBN 9781467159609

Library of Congress Control Number: 2025934732

CONTENTS

PENSACOLA: CITY OF FIVE FLAGS

Pensacola is the oldest European settlement in the United States, originally settled six years before the settlement of St. Augustine, Florida. The area has been governed under the authority of five different flags: Spain, France, Britain, the Confederate States of America and the United States. Sometimes control switched back and forth between nation states several times.

Each culture, including the Natives who have lived in the area for two thousand years, brought their culture with them. Food is a crucial part of every culture around the globe. Much has been written about the importance of food. It ties us to our homes, families and regional/national cultures. It gives us a sense of community. When people move to different parts of the globe, they keep their cooking traditions because it's the closest thing they can bring with them to tie them to their cultural roots. How many times have you heard friends lament, "I can't get pizza here like I did back home," or, "I miss New Jersey Italian food"? Let's not get started on the great barbecue debate.

Food is not monolithic. Each country around the globe has dishes that represent it as a whole. The United States has burgers, barbecue and much more. But region to region, state to state, things are prepared differently. North Carolina barbecue is vastly different than the barbecue found in Memphis. Fights have been started on the merits of boiled Gulf Coast crab versus steamed Maryland crab. It can get as bad as football rivalries.

Pensacola is and has been a melting pot for most of its existence. Each culture that moved here brought its culinary traditions and added them to the stewpot of our local cuisine. Spanish, French, British, Creole and African recipes started melding together. A Filipino community sprang up in Pensacola thanks to U.S. Navy servicemen marrying and bringing Filipino women back to the States and settling down in Pensacola. In the mid-1970s, the U.S. government placed thousands of Vietnamese refugees along the Gulf Coast from Brownsville, Texas, to the big bend of Florida. They were mostly fisherfolk who were able to escape Vietnam with their boats. Pensacola boasts numerous Asian grocery stores, and many have excellent authentic cafés attached that are brimming with people of all backgrounds slurping up giant bowls of pho noodle soup or attacking banh mi sandwiches with vigor.

Moving into the twenty-first century, Pensacola is becoming a rising star on the national food scene. It's getting noticed by food writers, magazines and newspapers from all over the United States and Canada. We have Food Network stars cooking in the downtown area. The no. 3 rated taco truck in the United States is located in a trailer behind a gas station off Interstate 10. Multiple chefs who have worked in Michelin Star restaurants have moved to the area. What's bringing them here is the quality of life. These chefs could go to Los Angeles; Washington, D.C.; or Miami and make much more money. In Pensacola, they can cook the food they want without the stresses of living and working in a major metropolitan city with cramped living spaces, small kitchens, heavy traffic, etc.

An amazing thing about the Pensacola food scene is that these chefs aren't in competition with each other. They are friends and socialize together. They hold each other up. What's really special is that many of them collaborate with each other and with local food trucks to create flavorful one-of-a-kind dishes. The cuisine runs the gamut: Northern Italian, Southeast Asian, German, Middle Eastern, Greek, Asian fusion, Creole/Cajun and Indian, and of course, there's fresh, local seafood of all kinds cooked in all ways.

For now, let us go back to the beginning.

1

THE FIRST PEOPLES

Humans first arrived in Florida between twelve thousand and fourteen thousand years ago during the last ice age. At that time, the peninsula of Florida was twice the size that it is today. The coastline in Pensacola was located many miles to the south of its current location. Escambia Bay started its life as a freshwater lake fed by the Escambia River and smaller tributaries. The people who meandered into the area were Paleolithic nomads, primitive hunter-gatherers who were following large game. At that time, large elephant-like mammoths were their primary source of food. Large now-extinct deer, sabertooth tigers and other mammals were on their menu. These nomadic bands had not yet discovered agriculture or primitive architecture, so they never stayed in one place for more than a few weeks. They would stalk large game, make a kill and camp near the kill site. Let's face it, once you down a mammoth, you aren't going to drag it anywhere. They would work down the carcass, making use of all they could—meat for eating, skin for clothing, sinew and bone for tools and weapons. Once they had extracted what they could—or when the carcass began to putrefy—they were off again, searching for more game. They would eat the berries, tubers and fruits they could gather while they camped or while on the march. These peoples eventually largely died out due to disease and warfare. It was a long time before humans arrived in North Florida again.

It was somewhere between 1000 BCE and 0 CE when people began wandering into the area. These were Neolithic people who were more

Native pottery discovered in downtown Pensacola on display at the Museum of History. *Author's collection.*

advanced than their predecessors. Still somewhat hunter-gatherers, these folks made pottery, had complex tools and lived in huts and basic log cabins with thatched roofs. They hunted and fished and had begun practicing limited, small-scale agriculture. They were planting what's known as the "Three Sisters": corn, beans and squash. The Three Sisters were staples for most tribes in North and Central America. They grew these crops close together on small plots. Corn grows straight up, and beans can wrap around the cornstalks to help save space. This allows squash to be planted directly underneath, helping keep weeds at a bare minimum. This style of growing is miraculous. Corn depletes the soil of nitrogen and beans add nitrogen to the soil, and both shade the squash, allowing it to flourish. It's amazing these semi-primitive people with no knowledge of modern science were able to figure this out such a long time ago.

Venison was about 50 percent of these peoples' dietary totals. Florida has small whitetail deer that numerously populated its woods. These primitive peoples would eat the deer fresh and smoke/dry it for consumption in the winter or for travel. Black bears were usually hunted in the winter. These peoples would use the bears for fat and oil and would use their skin/fur; however, bear was not a staple food. Squirrels, raccoons and rabbits were usually trapped in snares. Turkey and other fowl were hunted and eaten as well. Nuts and fall fruits rounded out these people's diets.

These tribes did not live on the coast for long periods. The soil around Pensacola is terrible. It's sandy, acidic and doesn't hold organic nutrients that feed vegetables. The tribes mostly lived forty to sixty miles north of Pensacola, around the present-day Florida-Alabama border. In the spring, they would plant their crops, and then some would vacation at the beach. They would travel south and place temporary fish camps along the bay, right in the heart of modern downtown Pensacola and northward, up into the Gull Point area.

In the state of Florida, in historic areas like downtown Pensacola, there is a law that says you cannot do any construction, demolition or digging without having a state archaeologist on site. Artifacts are still found today. On Bayfront Parkway, the Florida Power and Light (formerly Gulf Power) regional corporate office commands attention. It's a large, modern multistory brick and glass building located directly across the street from Pensacola Bay. Earlier in its history, this area was a neighborhood called Hawkshaw, where working-class people lived from the 1800s to about 1906. A hurricane in 1906 damaged much of the area, and it went into steep decline before it eventually disappeared.

In 1985, Dr. Judy Bense of the University of West Florida excavated the area before the construction of the Florida Power and Light building began. Her team found over one hundred trash pits that had not been mixed with the remains of later civilization. The archaeologists found over fifteen thousand pottery sherds and numerous food remains. Many fish bones of all kinds—mullet, speckled trout, pinfish, flounder, etc.—were found in the pits. These early civilizations also hunted in the area, as evidence of deer, turtle, alligator and otter bones were discovered. Thousands of oyster shells were also unearthed. These folks ate oysters like they would disappear the next day. Shucking knives didn't exist back then, so the oysters were placed in the cooking coals. The heat would roast them in the shell, and the oysters would pop open to be consumed. A roasted Pensacola oyster is a very fine thing.

Archaeologists also found the tools that were used to harvest the seafood. Fine meshed seine nets, traps, baskets, spears and bone fishhooks were discovered. It is likely they used canoes to harvest oysters, placed fish traps and hunted flounder. Blueberries, dewberries, persimmons, muscadines and scuppernong grapes grow wild and do well in Pensacola's terrible soil, and these fruits supplemented these early people's diets while they camped here.

In the late summer and early fall, the tribes would migrate back to their villages, harvest their vegetables and prepare for winter. They would periodically camp at the bay, although there could be many years in between their visits. But things permanently changed in the late fifteenth century.

EARLY TRIBAL RECIPES

Much research was done to identify the recipes that were used by the early peoples who inhabited this area. At that time, the tribes who lived in the Pensacola area had a more diverse and nutritious diet than their European commoner counterparts by making use of local fauna and flora. Meat was roasted over an open fire, smoked, dried and made into jerky and other foods. Because they were still quite primitive, they typically didn't have a meat with three sides. Most of their food was stewed in a pot. However, they did cook many different dishes. What follows are some recipes that were made by local tribes as best I can tell. Keep in mind that these peoples didn't have salt or seasoned broths—or many seasoning herbs at all so most of these recipes can be quite bland to the modern palette. These recipes are the basic foodstuffs that the tribes would have eaten up to two thousand years ago. Please feel free to add broths, salt and other seasonings as you please to your personal taste.

Acorns

Acorns are edible. Acorn flour is still used in cooking (albeit not much) to this day. Acorns are full of tannins and are quite bitter. Early on, the tribes would place them in woven sacks and leave them in a swift flowing creek for about two weeks to extract their bitterness. Later on, they devised a way to soak the acorns in wood ash and water. Acorn flour makes wonderful smallcakes and other baked goods. Acorn flour can be purchased online through any search engine. In the Southeast, oak trees are numerous, so there's free food everywhere, just lying on the ground. We will not go into foraging and preparing acorns here, as there are a few websites that will instruct you on how to do so if you wish to go that route. If you try to process acorns yourself, please follow all instructions carefully.

ACORN AND CORNMEAL CAKES

1 cup acorn meal
1 cup cornmeal
Water
$\frac{1}{4}$ cup honey
1 tablespoon melted butter or oil
A pinch of salt

Mix the ingredients with enough warm water to make a moist but not a sticky dough. Divide into balls. Cover and let the dough rest for ten minutes, or until ready to use. With moistened hands, pat the balls into thick tortillas. Heat an ungreased cast iron frying pan on medium-high heat. Place the cakes in the fryer. Cook until the edges start to get dry. When ready, flip them over and cook the other side until both sides are slightly brown

The Natives would have used rendered animal fat or oil instead of butter and would have cooked the cakes in ovens or on heated stones on a cookfire.

ACORN AND VENISON STEW

2 pounds venison, cut up
1 cup finely ground acorn meal

Cover the venison with water in pot or basket. Add hot rocks to simmer until the meat almost falls apart. Remove meat from the broth and chop into fine pieces. Return to pot with liquid and stir in acorn meal.

OR

Add the meat to a stewpot or slow cooker. Cover the meat with water and simmer for two hours on medium heat. Shred the meat with a fork and add acorn meal. Natives may have added squash and corn to the dish. You can also substitute beef for venison and beef, pork or chicken broth for added flavor.

CORN

Corn was the most important crop for almost every tribe in North America. An entire cookbook could be made of just corn recipes. The Natives consumed corn in many ways, from cornpone and hominy to succotash and more. Many times, it was added to stewpots either as whole kernels or as cornmeal to act as a thickener.

CORNPONE

Cornpone, or corncakes, were a staple food for the Natives. It's a simple dish made from corn flour and water. Sometimes, Natives would add cooked beans or fruits/berries and honey for added flavor. Modern recipes may use salt, baking powder and other ingredients, but these ingredients weren't available back then. The following is the basic recipe Natives used, albeit they are now baked in a modern oven rather than over hot stones.

Cornpone. *Author's collection.*

2 cups cornmeal
½ teaspoon salt
2 tablespoons melted butter or margarine
1½ cups (approximately) boiling water

Preheat oven to 375 degrees. Mix the cornmeal, salt and butter together, and add enough boiling water to make a semi-stiff dough. Using your hands, form small 4- to 6-inch hot dog bun shapes, and place them on a greased baking sheet. Bake at 375 for about 15 minutes or until edges start to brown. Let cool and eat.

Hominy

Hominy is a true Southern staple food. It is a dish of boiled corn kernels that ends up taking on a pasta-like texture. The Natives would soak dried corn kernels in an alkaline bath, usually of hardwood ash, to attain nixtamalization. This would give hominy a certain "hint of lime" flavor. Nixtamalization makes several otherwise unattainable essential amino acids and B vitamins digestible for humans. Non-nixtamalized hominy is not nutritionally complete, and European settlers who failed to nixtamalize their hominy caught "corn sickness" due to malnutrition, as they did not include beans to make a complete protein.

Making hominy at home is a very long and arduous process that we won't get into here; however, there are online sources and recipes should you wish to take on this endeavor. If you do, please do not use feed corn. It's treated with pesticides and fungicides. Canned hominy is available in most grocery stores in the Southeast, and that is what we will use here.

SAMP

Samp is a hominy porridge. It's made by cooking hominy with meat and beans in a stewpot. This is a slightly modern take on the original recipe.

4 (15½–ounce) cans white or yellow hominy
2 cans navy or cannellini beans*

Samp, a porridge made of hominy, beans and meat. *Author's collection.*

1 pound stew beef (the Natives would've used venison)
1 smoked pork hock (not authentic, but adds flavor)
1 medium onion, diced
2 cups water or broth

Combine all ingredients in a pot or Dutch oven, bring to a boil and then lower heat to medium/low and simmer for 1 hour. Add salt and pepper to taste.

**These beans are readily available. The types of beans the tribes grew in the area are difficult to find at the supermarket today. The Cherokee Trail of Tears beans would be the most similar to the type of beans that were used locally.*

SOFKEE

Sofkee can be either a drink or a soup and can be consumed hot or cold. It can be made with hominy or cornmeal; we will use cornmeal in this case. Sofkee tends to be sour, but it was a major dish that was enjoyed by the Natives in the Southeast, particularly in Florida.

3 quarts hominy
5 gallons water
1 pint ash lye

Place 3 quarts of hominy corn or grits into 5 gallons water. Add 1 pint of ash lye. Cook for 3 hours, or until the corn is tender.

This may be enjoyed warm or cold. After setting for a couple days, the mixture will become sour. Some enjoy adding honey as a sweetener.

Ash lye can be made at home, and there are many recipes online. The Seminole National Museum has sold it in the past, and it can possibly be obtained through them.

Pemmican, the original keto food. *Author's collection.*

PEMMICAN

Versions of pemmican were made by Native peoples all over North America. It's the original keto food. Pemmican is calorie and nutrient dense and lasts for a long time. It's perfect for winter consumption or for hunters on long trips. Pemmican is a food made from dried meat and fat. The meat is pounded into a powder and added to fat, usually venison or bison. For better nutrition and much better flavor, honey and berries may be added. The following is a version you can make at home.

2 pounds very lean meat (eye of round, top sirloin)
Up to 1 cup lard or beef tallow

Use the leanest cuts of meat from beef, bison, deer or elk. Adding berries or anything else will shorten the pemmican's shelf life. If you have any fat left over from harvesting, save it. If not, buy some rendered beef tallow or high-quality pork lard.

Slice the meat thinly, about ¼ to ⅓ inch thick. Remove any visible fat. Dry the meat in a dehydrator or oven by hanging the strips on oven racks as high as possible above the heating element. It can take up to and over 12 hours for the meat to dry.

Once the meat is dry, pulverize it into a powder. A food processor or grinder is preferable, or use a mortar and pestle if you're old-school. If you're adding berries, this is the time to do it, and dried berries are preferred.

Render the fat in a skillet until it's melted. Strain it through something like a cheesecloth to remove any crispy bits. In a bowl add the powdered meat and berry mixture. Add the fat to the mixture, just enough for the fat to soak into the powder. If you add too much fat too quickly, you may add some almond or flax meal to firm the mixture up. Once the mixture cools off, you may roll it into balls or cut it into bars. This is a pure protein/keto bar at its most basic and best, and it will keep for years (less so if you add berries). This isn't very tasty; it's utilitarian food. Feel free to jazz it up with curry powder and salt and pepper—get adventurous with your seasoning.

Cattail

This perennial plant is ubiquitous all over the southeastern United States and was a staple food for the tribes in this area. It is a hardy plant that thrives in marshy wetlands. Perhaps you've seen them growing along the highway in shallow ditches. Their look is unmistakable. The plant has a long stock and a "cat's tail" at its very end that looks like a corn dog. These plants have been dubbed "nature's supermarket," as their edible bits include their roots, shoots, immature flower heads, pollen and seeds. The roots can be ground into flour and contain 80 percent starch and up to 8 percent protein. It's a truly nutrient dense food.

CATTAIL POLLEN PANCAKES

Cattail pollen can be easily obtained online under the name "Pu Huang." Or if you prefer foraging it for yourself, there are numerous videos online that show how you can do just that. And it looks like it isn't difficult to do if you have the time and some cattails nearby.

1 cup flour
1 cup cattail pollen
2 teaspoons baking powder
1 teaspoon salt
2 eggs
2 cups milk
½ cup honey

Mix the dry ingredients together in a bowl, and add eggs, milk and honey. If the mixture is too thick, add a little water to thin it to pancake batter consistency. Heat a lightly greased griddle or skillet and add a dollop of the dough when it reaches the proper temperature (medium-high heat). Flip the dough halfway through cooking or when underside is slightly brown. Cook until both sides are slightly brown.

2

SPAIN ARRIVES

In 1492, Christopher Columbus arrived in the West Indies, and everything changed across the globe forever. At that point, Spain was the only coastal country in Europe that had the means to explore the New World. King Ferdinand II of Aragon married Queen Isabella I of Castille, thus uniting two powerful kingdoms to form one unified kingdom. Grenada, the last Muslim state in western Europe, had fallen, and Spain was unified and powerful and had great wealth. All the other European countries that had ships were involved in a conflict of some sort—either religious, civil or border wars—and they couldn't spare the money, ships or men to head west, so Spain had unrestricted access for a while.

Spain wasn't interested in empire-building at the time. It wanted more wealth, so gold, silver and jewels were its main goal in exploring the New World. The Aztecs, Incas, Mayans and other Central and South American civilizations had these goods in spades, so that's where Spain set up shop. Spaniards did search for gold throughout much of what was to become the southeastern United States. Much of Florida, Georgia, Alabama, Mississippi and even southern Arkansas was explored. Spanish conquistadors would find Native villages and then search for any tribespeople wearing gold or silver jewelry, which would indicate a source could be nearby. There are no precious metals anywhere in the Southeast, so the Spanish moved through and looked elsewhere. North America was of no use to them at that time due to its lack of suspected treasure.

The Gulf of Mexico can be unkind to ships, especially the sail-driven ships of that day. Hurricanes always have been and always will be a problem.

North Florida also gets severe thunderstorms regularly that can blow sixty-plus-mile-an-hour winds that can easily run a ship aground.

Over time, Spain was losing treasure ships to storms, and the golden age of piracy was just beginning. French and English corsairs like Sir Francis Drake were heading into the Atlantic and Caribbean Sea to raid Spanish treasure ships. Spain needed to alleviate that problem. It decided to build a colony somewhere on the Gulf Coast where it would then construct a road over land to a place called Santa Elena, where modern-day Parris Island, South Carolina, sits.

The viceroy of New Spain, Luis de Vasco, tapped his cousin Tristán de Luna y Arellano to head up the expedition. De Luna was a hidalgo (Spanish gentleman), a conquistador and a military commander. He chose the Bay of Ochuse (Pensacola Bay) as his landing spot. He gathered five hundred soldiers, one thousand colonists and a handful of clergy and set sail from Mexico. On August 15, 1559, eleven Spanish vessels entered the Ochuse's pass, sailed into the bay and anchored on Emanuel Point at the mouth of Bayou Texar. Just after arriving, De Luna sent one ship to Mexico and two ships to Spain to let them know they had arrived safely and were beginning to establish the colony.

Because the Spanish had just arrived and were beginning to fell trees for construction, they left their supplies on their ship. They had to live, sleep and cook on board until suitable housing was erected. There are records in Mexico City (the Spanish were notorious bureaucrats) of the food they brought. On the lists were cattle, pigs, goats/sheep and chickens. They also carried a dried rice/bean mixture called *manestra*, hardtack, flour, peaches and olives. They cooked on top of the deck in a *fogón*. Fogón stoves have been used in Spain for centuries. There was a cottage industry for shipboard fogóns that were cast iron boxes with three high sides and a lower front. The back parts of these fogóns had hooks and loops for utensils and sometimes a suspension arm for kettles. Sand was poured in the bottom, and a fire was lit on top. Most of what these Spaniards ate were stews. A fire was lit in the fogón, and water was heated. The manestra was added first to cook. Meat was added, and then the hardtack was included in the last ten minutes to thicken the stew and give it some heft. Leftovers from the night before were consumed at breakfast, and fruit with tortillas was eaten in the afternoon. The main meal was usually a stew. Since these Spaniards' rations weren't very diverse, there's not a lot of variety in the recipes from this time, but there's still a few things we can cook.

HARDTACK

Hardtack has been around for millennia. Just about every military, from North Africa to Scandinavia, on both land and sea, used hardtack as a staple of its diet. Hardtack is a very dry, hard bread that is made with literally just flour, water and sometimes salt. It's baked at a low temperature for several hours to remove all the moisture. Being so dry and dense, it can last for a very long time. How long? There is a piece of hardtack in a vacuum-sealed glass cube in the Smithsonian Institution that dates to 1863. This stuff lasts.

The Egyptians are credited with creating hardtack. They called it dhourra. *The Romans adopted it and called it ducellum, or bucellatum. It reached Europe during the Crusades and was called Muslim or muslin biscuit. Hardtack is too hard to eat when dry. It was also known by military men as "molar-breakers" and "tooth-dullers." It must be rehydrated to eat. It was mostly added to stews to make them more filling. The Spanish liked to break it up and soak it in wine before consuming it.*

Hardtack can be found in grocery stores, but it is uncommon. There are online stores that may ship it to you. The following is a basic recipe for hardtack.

2 cups all-purpose flour (do not use self-rising flour)
¾ cup water
1 ½ teaspoons salt (salt is optional, but it acts as a preservative)

Preheat oven to 375 degrees. Mix the flour, water and salt in a bowl. After it's mixed completely, the dough should be a little dry. If it's too sticky, add small amounts of flour until it becomes dry to the touch. Use a roller to spread out the dough on a counter or cutting board to reach a thickness of approximately ⅓ to ½ an inch. Cut the dough into 3-inch squares. Poke narrow holes in the hardtack biscuits with a chopstick or fork. The holes should go all the way through to the other side of the hardtack. This will prevent the crackers from puffing. Place the hardtack biscuits on a baking sheet and into the oven to bake for 30 minutes. Flip the hardtack over with a spatula and bake for another 30 minutes. Remove from oven, and using a spatula, flip the squares over and place back in oven at 375 degrees for another 30 minutes. Remove from the oven, and use a spatula to remove the hardtack from the baking sheet. Place the hardtack biscuits on a cooling rack to cool down. Once cooled, place the hardtack in an airtight container.

Remember, hardtack must be rehydrated in order to be eaten. It must be soaked for 5 to 10 minutes in liquid before it's eaten. The Spanish would break it up with their rifle butts and drop it into their stews or soak it in wine. One creative way to eat it is to smash it up into course bits and add sugar, hot water and whiskey to make a pudding.

BASIC FLOUR TORTILLA

Tortillas would have been used to mop/sop up stews, and they were traditionally used to cradle other foods.

2½ cups unbleached all-purpose flour
1 teaspoon baking powder
½ teaspoon salt
1 cup hot water (115–120 degrees)
3½ tablespoons extra virgin olive oil

In a medium-sized bowl, whisk together the flour, baking powder and salt. Add ⅞ cup of hot water and olive oil, and stir quickly with a fork or whisk to work the dough into a shaggy mass. Stir in additional water as needed to bring the dough together. Turn the dough out onto a lightly floured counter and knead briefly, just until the dough forms a ball. If the dough is very sticky, gradually add a bit more flour. Divide the dough into 8 pieces, then roll into balls, flatten slightly and allow them to rest, covered, for about 30 minutes.

While the dough rests, preheat an ungreased cast iron griddle or skillet over medium high heat, about 400 degrees. One at a time, roll a ball into an 8-inch diameter tortilla. Keep the remaining dough covered. Fry the tortilla in the ungreased pan for about 30 seconds on each side. Wrap the tortilla in a clean cloth when it comes off the skillet.

Repeat the process until all the dough is used, all while keeping the cooked tortillas covered.

De Luna's expedition was in this new spot for only five days when a massive and devastating hurricane struck the bay. They lost most of their ships, many people and most of their food. Within the next 2 years, things went from bad to worse to downright abysmal. Relief ships did arrive on scheduled visits, but many people starved, and oftentimes, the settlers had to rely on Natives for food, which strained their own food stores. After 2 years, it was decided the colony would be abandoned. In November 1561, the remaining settlers left the Bay of Ochuse, and no one but the Native tribes visited the bay for the following 137 years.

In 1698, Spain returned to the Bay of Ochuse. France had staked a claim in Mobile Bay (then known as Filipina Bay). Spain needed the closest deepwater port for a military installation to keep tabs on the French and hinder them from harassing their shipping lanes.

A fort was built on a bluff on the mainland across from the entrance of the pass, right about where Fort Barrancas sits on modern-day Pensacola Naval Air Station. It was called Presidio Santa Maria de Galve. It was a wooden stockade-style fort. A handful of professional soldiers and officers were posted to the fort, and some civilians joined in to start pig and cattle farms.

A small cooking pot found in a Spanish shipwreck off Emmanuel Point. One of De Luna's ships destroyed in the hurricane. *Author's collection.*

Olive pits. Over five hundred pits were recovered in the first of the three shipwrecks that were found, believed to be part of De Luna's lost fleet. *Author's collection.*

At that time, Spain didn't have much of a standing army, and very few volunteers offered to come to the back end of nowhere. The Spanish military cleaned out the jails in Mexico City to man the fort. These were street people—pickpockets, drunks, thieves, wastrels and garden variety low-level criminals. Florida had its own Botany Bay going on here. None of these folks had any useable skills, like farming, hunting or fishing, and the Spanish muskets weren't useful for hunting. British soldiers and British-allied Natives attacked the Spanish when they wandered into the interior to forage, so they were stuck inside the fort most of the time. Nearly all their food had to arrive via ship from Mexico in a shipment called the *situado*. It was all military rations, and none of it was healthy. Most food shipments consisted of salt pork, dried beef, dried rice and beans and six thousand pounds of hardtack. Sometimes, there would be sweet potatoes; plantains; honey; wine; a very rough, primitive rum called *aguardiente*; and peaches, if they were lucky.

Needless to say, this diet was really terrible. It had very little nutrition and was very low in vitamins and fiber, which meant almost everyone had scurvy. Tropical diseases were rampant. And this is not to mention that the situado was sometimes up to nine months late. Sometimes, it wouldn't arrive at all. Many times, when it did arrive, the food was bumped from the manifest to make room for other cargo or passengers. The fort was a hell on earth. Sometimes, the Spanish bought food from the well-supplied French in Mobile. This was not a place anyone wanted to be.

3
VIVE LA FRANCE

The year is 1719. The Spanish have been wallowing in misery in their little fort at the Bay of Ochuse for twenty-one years. A beleaguered Spaniard named Matamoras was the commander of the fort. He was likely sitting in his little cabin, writing his fiftieth report of the month, wishing he was anywhere else but here. Then something happens that he never, ever expected. Three French gunships appear in the pass and train their cannons on the fort. To make matters worse, four hundred Natives armed with French muskets, led by a troop of Canadian soldiers, surround the fort on the land side. Matamoras is confused, to say the least. There had recently been some skirmishes between the French and Spanish in the locality, but there had not an all-out invasion force. Turns out, France and Spain had declared war, but no one bothered to tell Matamoras what was going on. Knowing he wouldn't survive half a day under such withering firepower, Matamoras set up a parlay.

The Spanish surrendered the fort without firing a shot under two conditions. Firstly, the French had to leave the civilians alone. There were very few of them, and they were too busy trying to survive, concerned with raising their livestock, to be any threat to the French. Second, the French had to let the Spanish lay down their weapons and leave under military honors. The French relented, not wishing to battle if there was no need. Since the French wouldn't allow Spanish ships to enter the area, they took the Spanish on their ships and sailed to Cuba to release them. Once the Spanish left, the French occupied Presidio Santa Maria de Galve for the remainder of the war, which lasted only two years. When the war was over, the French decided to fall back to Mobile, Alabama, where they had a well-provisioned fort. As a last insult, the French burned the fort and any civilian homes near it to the ground to ensure the Spanish had nothing to come back to. Thanks, France.

Since the French occupied the one fort for only two years, their cooking influences at this time had no direct effect in Pensacola. That would change in thirty years.

4

SPAIN JUST WON'T QUIT

In 1722, hostilities ended between Spain and France. Gluttons for punishment, Spain decided to return to the Pensacola area, since France didn't want it. In all reality, it's a very strategic and easily defendable area and France didn't seem to care, so Spain decided to take advantage of the situation. Spain also needed a military installation close to the French to help guard their ships in that part of the Gulf of Mexico.

This time, Spain decided to build a fort on Santa Rosa Island, right about where modern-day Fort Pickens sits. Because who wouldn't want to live in a fort on the beach? So, Presidio Isla Santa Rosa was constructed. Its location was perfect to guard the pass, with heavy cannons pulled from warships and aimed at the pass and the gulf. This time, things were different for the folks who resided here. For starters, the area was a little more important to the Spanish Crown. Presidio Santa Rosa was set up as a way station for the Spanish fleet. Ships could anchor in Santa Rosa Sound behind the fort to make repairs using the abundant oaks and pines on the mainland. Fresh water was available from nearby creeks, and fresh pork and beef was available from the civilian haciendas on the mainland that the French didn't burn down.

This was a proper military installation, posted with professional soldiers and officers, and some military families were living with the soldiers in the fort. However, it was built on sand. You cannot grow things in sand. You cannot graze livestock on sand. So, aside from meat they were able to purchase from the civilians on the mainland, those at the fort still had to rely on supply ships from Mexico for most of their food. But these ships did arrive more regularly, and the supplies were of better quality than those the original Spanish garrison received a few years earlier.

It's surprising they lasted for thirty years on that little strip of sand at the mouth of the pass. However, after thirty years of hurricanes and high tides, the Spanish threw up their hands and said, "We're out!" They abandoned the fort in 1754 and moved to the mainland. Subsequent storms tore the fort to shreds, and there is nothing left of it now.

Previously, the Spanish had built a warehouse on the mainland. They usually had approximately nine soldiers posted on shore to guard it. They decided to build a fort around this warehouse, which was located on present-day Main Street, approximately where the Pensacola Cultural Center and UWF Museum of History currently sits. The western wall sat at Jefferson Street, right at Plaza Ferdinand, and ran north to present-day Government Street. The eastern wall was located right about where Tarragona Street sits today.

Presidio San Miguel de Panzacola was erected in 1754. Panzacola—sounds familiar. The Panzacola was a tribe of Natives who lived nearby. They were neither Creek nor Choctaw; rather, they were an independent tribe who were eventually assimilated into other tribes. *Panzacola* means "long haired people" or "hairy people" in their language. The Spanish were fond of naming settlements and places after the local peoples, partially because they were so brutal to the Natives during their exploratory phase, and they were attempting to placate them. But this didn't always work.

The Panzacola tribe did, in fact, live right on the bay at that time. Their territory stretched from present-day Fort Walton Beach on the western shore of Choctawhatchee Bay to the north end of Mobile Bay. There is a burial mound and museum located right in downtown Fort Walton Beach that once belonged to the Panzacola, and the Bottle Creek Indian Mounds, located at the heart of the Mobile-Tenesaw River delta, is the largest mound complex on the northern gulf coastal plain.

The Bay of Ochuse was now officially renamed Panzacola Bay. It's still not Pensacola though, is it?

Do you know how the name changed? Neither does anyone else. Local historians have a theory that makes a bucketful of sense. The Spanish monarchy and its nobility at the time were Castilians. Castilians have a different Spanish dialect from the rest of the Spanish-speaking world. They employ a lisp on their Ss and Zs. Barcelona and chorizo would be pronounced "Barthelona" and "choritho" by them. Panzacola was

Julee Cottage. Miss Julee was a free Creole businessowner who owned this cottage in the early 1800s. *Author's collection.*

probably pronounced "Panthacola." Dialects and accents change over time. Eventually, "Panthacola" morphed into "Pensacola." So, the city is most likely named after a mispronunciation. Go Florida.

At this time, some Creole peoples moved to the area. About forty Creole cottages dotted the woods near the fort, and those folks settled in and brought their cooking traditions with them. In time, these traditions had major influences in the daily diets of Pensacolians.

The cuisine was much better than the food the fort from 1698 enjoyed, but it was still very much based on military rations. The following are some foods they were most likely dining on. Notice the absence of seafood. The upper-class Spanish frowned on fish, as they believed it was peasant food, and they ate it only on Fridays and during Lent, when required to by the Catholic Church. Fish bones were excavated on the site where Presidio Panzacola sat, so we know they did catch and eat fish.

Author's note: Some of the following recipes lack an ingredients list. These Spanish recipes date to the medieval period and have been translated from the original Moorish and Spanish languages. It is up to the individual cook to determine the amounts of the ingredients needed, as none were given in the translations.

SEMOLINA BREAD

Hardtack would still have been dominant, as this was a military installation. However, flour would have been part of the situado, so these Spaniards would have been making breads as well. The bakers had their own starter cultures, but for modern convenience, we will be using prepared yeast.

2 packets (¼ ounce) yeast
3 cups lukewarm water
3 cups semolina flour (also known as durum flour)
3½ cups unbleached all-purpose flour
Salt to taste
¼ teaspoon cornstarch
¼ cup water

In a 5-quart bowl, mix the yeast with 3 cups of lukewarm water (about 102 degrees). Using a wooden spoon, mix in the flours and salt, little by little. Please use very wet hands to add the last bit of flour. No kneading is required.

Cover the dough loosely and allow it to rest at room temperature to rise for 2 hours. You may use the dough right away or store in the refrigerator. If storing, place the dough in a lidded—but not airtight—container and use in the next week.

When ready to use, dust the surface of the dough with all-purpose flour and cut off a 1-pound piece. Dust the dough with more flour and shape it into a ball by stretching the surface of the dough around to the bottom on all four sides, rotating the ball a quarter turn as you go. Form an oval- or round-shaped loaf. Place the dough on a flour-dusted board or pan and allow it to rest for 40 minutes.

Preheat the oven to 450 degrees 20 minutes before baking time, with a baking stone or heavy-duty sheet pan, inverted and preheated, placed on the middle rack. Place an empty broiler tray on a shelf that will not interfere with the rising bread. This will add moisture to your oven and will prevent your bread from forming a crust too soon.

Mix a cornstarch wash by blending the starch and water in a skillet. Boil for 30 seconds, or until the mixture appears "glassy." Cool completely.

Just before baking, paint the surface of the dough with the cornstarch wash, and slash the surface diagonally, using a serrated knife. Slide the loaf directly onto the hot stone or greased baking pan. Pour 1 cup of hot tap water into the broiler tray and quickly close the door to trap the steam.

Bake the bread for about 30 minutes, or until the crust is golden brown and firm to the touch. Cool on a rack before serving.

LOAF FRIED IN HONEY AND BUTTER (HONEY SAFFRON LOAF)

This recipe is taken directly from the Anonymous Andalusian Cookbook, *written by an anonymous author. The book was compiled by an unknown scribe in the 1400s. The book contains recipes copied from a number of older works from the 1200s to the 1400s.*

Sift white flour 3 times. Take the choicest part, mingle it with butter and knead it with egg yolk. Put into the dough some saffron and salt to form a round loaf.

Put clarified butter into an earthenware frying pan, boil it and take 1 part of honey to 1 part of dough (equal portions) and put them into the melted butter until the loaf is cooked. Before it is fully cooked, put on blanched almonds or pine nuts. Sprinkle with black pepper and present it.

MURRI

Murri was essential to Andalusian cooking during that period. Much like soy sauce, it was used as a flavor-enhancing condiment. It is high in glutamines, which gives it a strong umami flavor. Murri was made by fermenting barley dough wrapped in fig leaves. The following describes how it was prepared during the period, but you may use soy sauce as a substitute, since the flavor is very similar.

Blend raw barley with unbleached all-purpose flour and enough water to make a firm dough. Wrap in dry fig leaves and store in a dry place for 40 days to ferment. After 40 days, grind the dough, mix it with water and salt and more flour, and store in a fermenting crock for another 40 days. At the end of this period, it should look like a mahogany-colored paste. Add water to dissolve to form murri.

A quicker (and more sanitary method) is to mix 2 parts barley flour to 1 part salt to make a loaf that is baked in the oven until it is hard (like hardtack) and then pounded into crumbs. Then it's soaked in water for a day and night and then strained and set aside. This is known as the "first murri." Murri was frequently flavored with additives. Raisins, carob, dill, fennel, citron, sesame, anise, mace and other things were boiled in pine seed milk and water and then strained. This was known as "second murri." This was added to the first murri and boiled until thickened. Add to dishes like you would soy sauce.

HOW RICE IS COOKED IN THE EAST

This recipe is also from the Anonymous Andalusian Cookbook. *The Moors brought rice and chickpeas to Spain in the Middle Ages. Dried rice was brought to the New World by the Spanish and was always on the menu in new Panzacola area starting in 1698.*

Take rice washed with hot water and put it in a pot. Add fatty beef from the chest, hind parts, waist and leg bones. Add water to cover, plus a little more, and sufficient salt. Place in the bread oven overnight and take out the next morning. When it is all mushy, turn it onto a platter and sprinkle it with cinnamon, ginger and brown sugar.

ROYAL JASHISHA: IT FATTENS THIN WOMEN AND MEN

This is also taken from the Anonymous Andalusian Cookbook.

Take crushed wheat and an equal amount of rice and garbanzo beans (dried) with spices. (We are assuming the spices available could have been sweet—ginger, cinnamon, anise—or more savory, like the ras el hanout blend). Place this all in a pot. Cover with water and cook until it's completely done. Adjust it with a little salt. And so this is delicate, like a hasa (soup), pour on fresh butter and melted fat and the broth of a young, fat meat. Then sip it, because this increases one's strength greatly.

TORTOISE PIE

There is archaeological evidence that turtle and gopher tortoises were eaten in the Pensacola area beginning several thousand years ago BCE. Bones have been found in excavations in the area. The following is a recipe from the Anonymous Andalusian Cookbook *for tortoise or mullet pie.*

Simmer tortoise meat lightly in water with salt, and then remove from water. Add a little murri (use soy sauce) pepper, cinnamon, olive oil, onion juice, cilantro and a little saffron. Beat it all with eggs. Arrange the tortoise or mullet meat in a pie crust and throw it over the egg filling. The pastry should be kneaded with pepper and oil and brushed on when it is nearly done. Add saffron.

It is not known if cilantro was used in Pensacola at the time, but it was being used in Mexico, so we can assume it may have been shipped here as well. If not, leave it out of the recipe to make it more authentic.

A ROAST OF MEAT

Chop the meat of a young animal into chunks; add spices and cumin and the same amount of thyme, chopped garlic and vinegar. Marinate a little while (30 minutes to 1 hour) and roast on a spit, basting with oil and murri (use soy sauce) and eat.

ANOTHER ROAST OF MEAT

Roast salted, well marbled meat (cut up) like fingertips. Put in a pot (with water) spices, onion, salt, olive oil and soaked garbanzo beans. Cook until done. Then add the roast meat. Cover the contents of the pot with cilantro and sprinkle with pepper and cinnamon.

HIMMASIYYA (HUMMUS WITH MEAT)

Dried garbanzo beans would have been a staple of the diet at Presidio Panzacola. This is a dish they would have made. Do not use canned beans or prepared hummus. This dish needs to be cooked as follows.

2 cups dried garbanzo beans
1 pound diced pork
1 tablespoon salt
¼ cup red wine vinegar
1 head garlic, chopped
¼ cup olive oil
1 teaspoon powdered cinnamon
1 teaspoon ground ginger
¼ teaspoon ground black pepper
¼ teaspoon ground cloves
1 tablespoon dark brown sugar

Soak garbanzo beans overnight, rinse and then grind them with a potato masher or food processer. Do not overgrind, as the mix needs to be coarse.

Place meat in a pot, cover with water and place on a stove over high heat. Add garbanzo mix to the pot. Add salt, red wine vinegar, one head chopped garlic and olive oil, then mix all contents and bring to a boil.

Once boiling, lower heat to a simmer and let cook for 45 minutes. Once cooked, add powdered spices and dark brown sugar, cool and serve.

Hummus with roasted meat. *Author's collection.*

PORK AND BEANS WITH RICE

It's no secret the Spaniards are mad about pork. They even have a museum dedicated to it. That's hardcore. The Spanish introduced pigs to Florida, as no native species lived there. Some hogs managed to escape, either by slipping their pens or getting loose during storms, and flee into the interior. There were virtually no natural predators for the pigs, so they bred like crazy. All wild hogs in Florida are descendants of the Iberian pork the Spaniards brought with them. They are considered an invasive species, so if you own land in Florida and wild hogs are on it, they are considered nondomestic livestock and are your property to do with as you wish. There are laws for hunting hogs on state-managed land, however.

When the Moors conquered Spain in the early 1700s, they outlawed the consumption of pork, as it goes against the Islamic halal diet. When Spain forced the Moors out in the early 1500s, pork consumption came back with a vengeance.

150 grams dried garbanzo beans
1 onion
2 bay leaves
1 head garlic
½ kilogram fresh pork belly
2 leeks
4 cups (1 liter) of red wine
½ cup (100 grams) brown sugar
240 grams long rice
2 garlic cloves
Olive oil
Pepper to taste
Salt to taste
Scallions (optional, for garnish)

Soak beans overnight; in the morning, rinse, drain and separate any bad beans. Peel and roughly chop an onion and place it in a pot of water (6 cups) on the stove. Add bay leaves, head of garlic and beans to water. Bring to a boil, skim top when needed, reduce to a simmer and cook for 90 minutes. Turn off heat, remove garlic and bay leaf.

Clean the pork belly and wash and chop the leeks and onion. Brown the pork belly in skillet with oil and remove. Sauté leeks and onion in the

Pork and beans with rice. *Author's collection.*

remaining pork fat. Place the pork belly with the leek and onion in a Dutch oven, cover with wine and add sugar and bay leaf. Cover and roast for 1 hour at 280 degrees.

Cook rice, thinly slice 2 garlic cloves and add to cooked rice.

Remove pork from oven and allow to cool. Slice pork belly into cubes, add to bowl with beans and rice, and add a little wine/bean water if you wish. Garnish with chopped scallions.

SOFRITO

Sofritos are found all over the former Spanish empire. With origins in Spain and probably Italy (Romans—is there anything they didn't influence?), sofrito is an aromatic vegetable base used to enhance other dishes (think murri or soy sauce). The Spanish, particularly in the New World, ate tomatoes, whereas the rest of Europe took a very long time to adapt to the "devil's fruit." Each region has its own variation of sofrito; this one would've been used in Spain itself, as well as Northwest Florida.

½ cup (120 milliliters) extra-virgin olive oil
5 medium cloves garlic, minced

4 medium yellow onions, finely diced
2 large green peppers, stemmed, seeded and finely diced
1 leek, white and light green parts only, washed well and finely diced
Salt to taste
2 tablespoons (30 milliliters) tomato paste

In a 3-quart saucepan, heat oil over medium-high heat until shimmering. Add garlic, onions, green peppers and leek. Season lightly with salt and cook, stirring, until vegetables have released their liquid and are beginning to brown lightly on the bottom of the pan, about 10 minutes. Lower heat to medium-low and continue cooking, stirring and scraping frequently, until sofrito is sweet to the taste and a deep golden-brown color, about 45 minutes. Stir in tomato paste and cook for 2 minutes. This should yield 2 cups and can last up to five days when refrigerated.

Sofrito, a flavor enhancer for soups, stews and rice or bean dishes. *Author's collection.*

SPANISH ROASTED PORK

The king of the dinner table. This is a very common recipe that would have been cooked in the Pensacola area. There were haciendas on the mainland that supplied Presidio Isla Santa Rosa with fresh pork, so this would have been a common meal.

4 cups salt water (for washing pork)
¼ cup vinegar or lime juice (for washing pork)
1 (6-pound) pork shoulder
12 garlic cloves
2 tablespoons olive oil
1 teaspoon ground black pepper
2 tablespoons salt
1 teaspoon dried oregano
2 tablespoons vinegar
2 tablespoons Sazón Tropical® (or 1 teaspoon each coriander, cumin, annatto and garlic powder)
2 tablespoons sofrito
1½ to 2 cups water

Wash pork shoulder in salt water and vinegar or lime juice, clean thoroughly, rinse and pat dry. Cut slits into the pork shoulder, both front and back, 1 to 2 inches wide and 2 to 3 inches deep. The slits should be wide and deep enough to fill with the sofrito and garlic halves.

Take 6 whole garlic cloves, as well as olive oil and place into a mortar and pestle, or pilon, and crush and infuse olive oil with garlic. After the ingredients are crushed, add ground black pepper, salt, oregano, vinegar and Sazón Tropical® seasoning to the mortar and pestle, and combine all the ingredients until it becomes a paste, set aside.

Put sofrito into the slits or cuts in the pork shoulder, both front and back. Stuff the other half of the garlic cloves into the pork shoulder.

Take the mashed spice mixture and rub all over pork shoulder. Allow the pork to marinate for 1 to 24 hours in the refrigerator before roasting it in the oven.

When the pork is ready to cook, cover with aluminum foil or place in a roasting pan. Before roasting, add 1½ to 2 cups of water into the pan. Place pan in the oven and bake for 3 to 3½ hours. After the second hour, remove the pork from the pan and place on an oven rack. Place the roasting pan with the liquid or juices under the pork to catch further drippings. Rotate the pork until it's completely roasted (reaches an internal temperature of 145 degrees).

Once the pork is fully roasted, allow it to sit for about 15 minutes before carving.

ROASTED SWEET POTATOES

Sweet potatoes were part of the military rations in Spain's second foray into Northwest Florida and were eaten at Presidio Santa Maria de Galve. Still on the menu in the 1740s, sweet potatoes would have been regularly eaten in Presidio Panzacola.

2 teaspoons cumin
2 teaspoons paprika
1 teaspoon chili flakes
1 teaspoon salt
2 cloves garlic, crushed or grated

3 tablespoons olive oil
Juice of 1 lime
1 large sweet potato, chopped into half-inch cubes

Preheat your oven to 425 degrees. Mix together cumin, paprika, chili flakes, salt, garlic, olive oil and lime juice in a large bowl. Add the cubes of sweet potato and stir to coat thoroughly. Place the sweet potato cubes on a large nonstick baking tray, ensuring the cubes are well spread out in a single layer. Roast in the oven for 20 minutes.

THREE MEATBALL DISHES

ALSO TAKEN FROM THE *ANONYMOUS ANDALUSIAN COOKBOOK*

The Spanish would've taken cuts of chuck, round and other bits, free of tendons, etc., and pounded them with rough cleavers until they resembled a rough ground/paste-like consistency.

1 pound ground beef
¼ teaspoon cumin
¼ teaspoon coriander
¼ teaspoon black pepper
Pinch saffron
2 eggs
1 tablespoon vinegar
1 tablespoon olive oil
Murri (use soy sauce)
1 clove chopped garlic

DISH 1

To the ground beef, add cumin, coriander, pepper and saffron, and beat one egg into mixture. Knead together and roll into meatballs. In a clean pot, add 1 tablespoon of olive oil, 1 tablespoon of vinegar, a dash of murri and garlic.

Brown meatballs in mixture over medium high heat. Reduce heat to low, cover and cook for an additional 30 minutes.

Remove from heat and cover contents with beaten egg, saffron and pepper and let congeal. You may wish to dye the dish a certain color. Cilantro or mint juice can be used to turn it green, saffron can turn it yellow and almonds can make it white.

DISH 2

Make meatballs as instructed for dish 1, and put them in a pot on high heat with olive oil. Add 1 tablespoon of vinegar, 1 tablespoon murri, 1 onion (pounded with ¼ cup cilantro), salt, a pinch of ground thyme, 1 clove of chopped garlic, chopped parsley thyme and water (about ½ cup) to braise.

Add 3 beaten eggs and let cook until eggs are fully cooked. Ladle out, sprinkle with cinnamon, pepper and parsley.

DISH 3

Make meatballs as instructed for dish 1, only half their size. Grill on a spit of hot coals until they are browned and place on a platter. Cut them into pieces and season with murri (soy sauce).

CHICKEN (ANOTHER GOOD DISH)

ALSO TAKEN FROM THE *ANONYMOUS ANDALUSIAN COOKBOOK*

2 tablespoons olive oil
2 tablespoons murri (soy sauce)
1 teaspoon coriander seeds
1 teaspoon thyme
Salt and pepper to taste
1 bunch cilantro
1 medium onion, chopped
1 pound ground chicken
1 medium egg

Heat a pot with olive oil, murri, coriander seeds, thyme, pepper, cilantro and onion. Add ground chicken and cook until chicken is browned. Pour in enough water to cover the meat and cook for 10 minutes on high. Take ground meat and mix with breadcrumbs, pepper and raw egg. Cover and heat until egg is fully cooked (low heat).

RICE AND BEANS

Dried rice and beans (known as manestra) were staples of Spanish military rations. When stored correctly, they could last for years, making this a nutritious meal filled with needed carbohydrates, protein and fiber.

3 cups (710 milliliters) vegetable broth
¼ cup (65 milliliters) extra-virgin olive oil
1 potato
½ onion
4 cloves garlic
1 green bell pepper
2 tomatoes
1 teaspoon sweet smoked Spanish paprika
1 cup uncooked rice
1 (15½-ounce) can chickpeas
Salt and pepper to taste
Handful chopped fresh parsley

Add 3 cups (710 milliliters) of vegetable broth to a saucepan and heat over a medium-high heat. Heat a large fry pan over a medium-high heat and add in a generous ¼ of cup olive oil.

Cut 1 potato into ¼-inch-thick rounds.

Heat the oil for 2 minutes; add in the slices of potato, making sure they're all in a single layer, and cook for 4 to 5 minutes per-side.

While the potatoes are cooking, roughly dice ½ onion, chop 4 cloves garlic, thinly slice a bell pepper (seeded and deveined) and finely chop tomatoes. After cooking the slices of potato for 8 minutes (4 minutes per side), remove from the pan and set aside.

Using the same pan with the same heat level, add diced onions and strips of bell pepper, mix with the olive oil. After 3 minutes, once the veggies are lightly sauteed, add in the chopped garlic, mix and cook for 30 seconds. Then add in 1 teaspoon of sweet smoked paprika, quickly mix together and then add in the chopped tomato and simmer for 2 minutes. Allow tomato to thicken into a sauce-like consistency, and then add in 1 cup of uncooked rice and a can of chickpeas and season with salt and black pepper. Mix together until well combined, and then add in the hot vegetable broth. Give it 1 final mix and then add the fried potatoes back into the pan in a single layer. Simmer for 9 to 10 minutes until most of the broth has been absorbed but there is still a little bit left. Then lower the heat to a low-medium heat and simmer for another 3 to 4 minutes, or until all the broth has been absorbed. Let sit for 20 minutes to allow rice to finish absorbing the liquid. Garnish with chopped parsley.

BRAISED PORK SHANK

Pork shanks are delicious and cheap cuts of the walking menu that is the noble pig. There are many refined recipes from gourmet chefs that uses lots of frou-frou ingredients the Spanish wouldn't have had access to or the time to make. This is a basic recipe that would've been made in the presidio with the fresh pork that was available from colonists on the mainland.

¼ cup olive oil
4 pork shanks
1 large onion, chopped
2 cups red wine
6 cups water (can use chicken or ham stock/broth)
Sprig rosemary
Several bay leaves
Sprig thyme
6 cloves garlic, sliced
Salt and pepper to taste
¼ cup chopped parsley

Put a large lidded pot over medium-high heat and add olive oil. Add and brown pork shanks on all sides, or for about 10 minutes. Remove and set aside.

Lower heat to medium, add onions and sauté until soft, or for about 10 minutes. Add wine and simmer until reduced by ¼.

Add pork shanks back into pot, add water (or broth) and make sure shanks are mostly submerged in the liquid. Add rosemary, bay leaves, thyme, garlic, salt and pepper. Cover and simmer over medium heat for 2½ hours, turning shanks every 30 minutes.

Remove pork and serve over rice or chickpeas. If you want to get swanky, remove the garlic and herbs and continue cooking the liquid until it reduces by half. Then spoon off the surface fat and add gravy to the pork. Garnish with chopped parsley.

GARUM

Garum is an ancient food that dates to Roman times, as it was the Romans who brought the recipe to Spain. It is a highly salty fish sauce and is used as a flavoring condiment much like the previously listed murri. It is a very easy recipe to follow, as it requires only two ingredients, fish and salt. It has an umami characteristic to it, and a little goes a long way. This is a fun recipe to make on your own if you can get fish that is very fresh. If not, just go to the international section of your local supermarket and buy some bottled fish sauce—it's the same thing.

The original primitive garum recipe used by the Romans consisted of adding salt to fish in jars and leaving it in the hot Mediterranean sun for days on end so it would ferment and liquefy. The following is a stovetop version that is quicker to make, but it tastes the same.

2 pounds small fish (must be fresh, sardines, smelt, anchovies and/or smelt; must remain whole, as the innards are part of the flavoring agents that make this sauce what it is)
500 grams salt (kosher, pickling or sea salt)
2¾ pints water

Place the fish and salt in a pan on the stovetop, add water to cover the fish with 2 inches overhead and bring to a boil. Boil for at least 15 or 20 minutes. Then reduce the heat and crush the fish with a fork or wooden spoon (make sure these utensils are very clean). Bring the mix back to a boil until it thickens—this could take up to 30 minutes but probably less, so keep an eye on it.

To begin the straining process, start with a coarse strainer and mash the mixture with the back of a wooden spoon with the liquid going into a clean bowl. Repeat the process through a cheese cloth or a paper towel until the liquid is clear. It should end up being a light amber color with no solids in it. Place in a sterilized bottle or jar.

This garum is not very fishy tasting and is less bold than its Asian counterpart, as it's not fermented.

FERMENTED GARUM

5 pounds small fish (must be fresh, sardines, smelt, anchovies and/or smelt; must remain whole, as the innards are part of the flavoring agents that make this sauce what it is)
1½ pounds salt (kosher, pickling or sea salt)
2¾ pints water

Same as the unfermented garum, start with about 5 pounds of small fish, rinsed but intact, placed in a clean container that will hold that amount. Add 1½ pounds of salt and thoroughly mix it with the fish. You may add potent herbs like coriander, mint, fennel or oregano in this process. Let this mix sit in the sun (sealed) for 7 days. Then mix the sauce daily for 20 days. Strain the liquid as described in the previous recipe.

5

RULE, BRITANNIA

While Presidio Panzacola was sleeping away in the balmy North Florida climate, big things were happening elsewhere around the globe. In 1756, the Seven Years' War broke out. In a nutshell, European empires and their allies were seeking to expand their global dominance, and fighting happened all over the planet. The French and Indian War in North America was a part of this conflict. Spain allied itself with France. Hostilities ended in 1763, with Britain and their allies victorious. In one of the many Treaties of Paris, Spain ceded the territory of Florida to Britain in exchange for Spain reclaiming Cuba, which the British had conquered during the war.

Now, Pensacola was under the third of its five flags.

In 1764, the Brits moved into Presidio Panzacola. At that time, the fort and village looked like a slum. According to a report written by British Captain Wills, the town at that time consisted of "40 huts, thatched with palmetto leaves, and barracks for a small garrison, the whole surrounded by a stockade of pine posts." Wills went on to describe the terrain:

> *The country, from the insuperable laziness of the Spaniards, still remains uncultivated. The woods are still near the village, and a few paltry gardens show the only improvements. Stock, they have none, being entirely supplied by Mobile, which is pretty well cultivated and produces sufficient for export.*

The British decided to change all of that. Instead of a backwoods military post, Pensacola was destined to become, in the British eyes, a proper city. They saw the unbridled potential of the area, with its abundant natural

Left: A placard on excavated kitchen from the British era of Presidio Panzacola. *Author's collection.*

Below: A replica hearth in a 1700s outdoor kitchen in the Historic Village. *UWF Historic Trust, Downtown Pensacola; author's collection.*

resources. Soon, Pensacola became a small but burgeoning economic center. One major thing the British did was city planning. They brought in an urban planner named Elias Durnford, who laid out a plan for growth. What is now downtown Pensacola was soon established by an urban grid layout. All the streets ran due north, south, east and west in straight lines. They built out the streets for future expansion, so when they needed to add more buildings, the streets were already there.

Soon, career military people and their families, land speculators, shipbuilders, lumber businesspeople, shipping companies and mercantile companies moved into the quickly growing area, and Pensacola became a proper town. It was no longer just a military installation. This meant the food drastically changed. Things from all over the British empire began arriving in Pensacola. Tea, spices, cookware and tableware all began pouring in, and British cooking was now the rule of the day. Creoles still lived in the area, and they will be discussed a little later. There were also some Spaniards and French folk living here, as they were conducting trade.

My grandparents owned Wesley's Refrigeration and Heating for many decades on Tarragona Street, across from the old Pensacola News Journal (now the Southtowne Apartments). Currently, there are some brick townhomes on the spot. That was the original location of the First United Methodist Church, founded in 1821, and there were English houses on that plot before that. I found the remains of a trash pit on that location back in the day. In that area, I found broken bits of porcelain that were once part of a tea set, as well as some other pieces of pottery from the era. A British merchant would have transported it from Britain, and a colonist would have brought it to Pensacola. It was then broken and tossed out where I was lucky enough to find it over a century later. The pieces are sitting in my curio cabinet as you read this.

The British are widely known for three things: their empire spread on the back of a highly organized and efficient merchant society, an effective military and gardening. The Brits can grow flowers in a snowstorm. If you ever find yourself in the historic residential district in the southeastern part of downtown Pensacola, you will notice the homes are right on top of each other, and there are barely any yards to speak of. The Brits wanted gardens—badly. Under the original planning of Elias Durnford, each home was issued a free companion piece of ground to the north border of the town. According to Pensapedia,

> *The lots on the south side of the street had an area of 80 feet front and 170 in depth. North of that street they were 192 feet square, known as*

Top: Kitchen implements from the 1700s. *Author's collection.*

Bottom: Replica kitchen washing sink from the 1700s. *Author's collection.*

> *arpent or Garden lots, and numbered to correspond with those lying south of the street, which were, strictly speaking, town lots. In order to furnish each family with a garden spot, each grantee of a town lot was entitled, upon the condition of improvement, to receive a conveyance of an arpent lot of the same number as his town lot.*

These lots were free to sovereign British citizens. Spanish, French and Creole citizens weren't allowed to take advantage of these lots. The British, being excellent gardeners, could fertilize and compost the terrible soil into submission in order to yield food. They cultivated vegetables, grew citrus trees (the Spanish had introduced the Seville orange to Pensacola previously; some wild descendants of those original orange trees still grow in downtown Pensacola), raised goats for milk or just grew flowers. The vegetables grown weren't enough to feed the town, so most vegetables were bought from the Mobile area to the west.

These gardens were where Garden Street got its name.

British cuts of meat and sausages and, of course, British baking were now the rule of the day. Cookbooks from England would've arrived in Pensacola with the new colonists. Titles like *The New and Easy Method of Cookery*; *The Compleat Housewife, or Accomplished Gentlewoman's Companion 9th Edition*; *The Experienced House-Keeper, For the Use and Ease of Ladies*; and *English Housewifry* would've been used in Pensacola at that time. The following recipes are compiled from those books.

TO MAKE SCOTCH SOOP

1 beef shank
1 sheep or goat neck
1 pound barley
6 quarts water
1 plucked and gutted chicken
Green vegetables (collards, mustard, turnip)
3 spring onions, chopped

Take a houghil of beef (shin shank), cut it into pieces with a neck of mutton (sheep didn't fare well in the North Florida climate, so goat would've been used) and 1 pound of barley. Put them all into your pot with 6 quarts of water. Bring to a boil until the barley is soft; then put in a fowl (chicken or dove). As soon as it is cooked enough, put in a handful of green vegetables (whatever was grown) and blades of onions. Let them have only a little boil; otherwise, it will spoil the greenness. Serve it up with the fowl in the dish, garnished with the raspings of bread.

TO STEW A BRISKET OF BEEF

1 beef brisket, any size
Ground mace to cover brisket
Salt and pepper to taste
8 beef broth bones
Bouquet garni thyme, sage, basil mint, rosemary
1 white onion
Sweetbreads (chicken gizzards, hearts)
1 chicken
¼ pound mushrooms
Claret
1 lump butter
Flour

Take the thin part of a brisket of beef, score the skin at the top, cross and take off the under skin. Then take out the bones and season it heavily with mace, a little salt and a little pepper. Rub it on both sides, and then let it lie at night (for the Lord's sake, if you do this, place it in the refrigerator—I believe they had stronger immune systems back then).

Make broth of the bones, skim the fat clean off, add as much water as it takes to cover it well and let it stew over a slow fire for four or five hours with a bunch of sweet herbs and an onion cut into quarters. Turn the beef over every hour, and when you find it to be tender, take it out of that broth and drain it very well, having made a little good, strong gravy.

Add a ragoo with sweetbreads cut in pieces; pullet (chicken) tenderly boiled and cut in long pieces; mushrooms, if you have any; and a little claret, and throw in your beef. Let it stew 1 hour in the ragoo, turning it over sometimes. Take out your beef and thicken your ragoo with a lump of butter and a little flour.

TO BOIL DUCKS WITH ONION SAUCE

2 ducks
4 or 5 large white onions
2 cups milk
4 cups water
2 tablespoons butter
Salt and pepper to taste

Take 2 fat ducks and season them with pepper and salt. Skewer them at both ends and boil them while they are tender. Take 4 or 5 large onions and boil them in milk and water, changing the water 2 or 3 times in the boiling. When they cooked are enough, chop them into very small pieces and run them through a sieve with the back of a spoon. Melt a little butter and put it in your onions with a little salt, and then pour it upon your ducks.

TO BOIL CHICKENS

4 or 5 small chickens
½ gallon milk
1 gallon water
Pinch salt

Take 4 or 5 small chickens, as you would have your dish in bigness. If they are small chickens, you may scald them, as this will make them whiter; draw them and take out the breastbone before you scald them. When you have dressed them, put them in milk and water and wash them, truss them and cut off the heads and necks. Boil them in milk and water with a little salt. Half an hour or less will boil them.

TO MAKE A SAUCE FOR THE BOILED CHICKENS

Offal from chickens (gizzards livers, necks, hearts)
Water to cover
Vegetable pickle

Spoonful cream
Lemons
Butter
Flour

Take the necks, gizzards and livers and cover with water and boil; when they are cooked enough, strain off the gravy and put them into a vegetable pickle. Take the livers, break them into small pieces and mix in a little gravy and strain through a sieve with the back of a spoon. Put in a spoonful of cream and grated lemon peel, and thicken it with butter and flour. Pour on your chickens and garnish with lemon.

TO MAKE A FRICASEY OF TRIPES

2 pounds honeycomb beef tripe
1 lemon, juice and zest
1 tablespoon white wine
3 egg yolks
¼ cup heavy cream
¼ cup shredded parsley
2 or 3 chives, chopped
Lemon slices for garnish
Sliced mushrooms to cover

Take the whitest and thickest seam tripe you can get, cut the white part into thin slices and put it into a stew pan with a little white gravy, the juice of a lemon and lemon peel shred (zest)—also a spoonful of white wine. Take the yolks of 2 or 3 eggs and beat them very well. Add to them a little thick cream, shredded parsley and 2 or 3 chives and shake over the stove while it is as thick as cream, but don't let it boil for fear that it will curdle. Garnish your dish with lemon and sliced mushrooms.

WHITE GRAVY FOR SOUPS OR SAUCE

1 pound beef knuckle (sirloin tip)
6 quarts water
1 whole mace
2 tablespoons black peppercorns
10 whole cloves
Salt to taste

Take a knuckle of beef and boil it in 6 quarts of water until it strings; then strain it. Before it is half-boiled, put in whole mace, pepper, cloves and salt to keep it for use. You can make the gravy of mutton the same way.

HOW TO COLLAR A PIECE OF BEEF TO EAT COLD

5 pounds beef brisket
2 ounces saltpeter (sodium nitrate)
2 ounces salt
Bouquet garni basil, thyme, oregano, rosemary, sage (shredded)
2 pounds bacon
Greens
1 tablespoon powdered mace
1 teaspoon black pepper
1 tablespoon nutmeg
Anchovy (optional)
5 bay leaves
Jamaica pepper
Black pepper
1 quart stale beer
¼ cup vinegar

Take a plank of beef, bone it and take off the inner skin. Nick your beef about an inch long, but mind that you don't cut through the skin on the outside. Then take 2 ounces of saltpeter and beat it small; then take a large handful of common salt and mix them together, first sprinkling your beef over with a little water. Lay it in an earthen dish and sprinkle over your salt; then let it stand 4 or 5 days. Then take a large quantity of all sorts of mild sweet herbs, and pick and shred them to very small pieces. Take some bacon and cut it into long pieces the thickness of your finger; then take your beef and lay one layer of bacon in every nick, and then place another of greens. When you have finished this, season your beef with a little beat of mace, pepper, salt and nutmeg; you may add a little anchovy in the nicks. So, roll it tight, and bind it in a cloth with a course inkle round it; then put it into a large stew pot and cover it with water. Let the beef lie with the end downward, and put to it the pickle that was in the beef when it was in salt; then set it into a slow oven for the night. Then take it out and bind it tight, tying up both ends. The next day, take it out of the cloth and put it in to pickle; you must take the same pickle it was baked in, take off the fat and boil the pickle. Put in a handful of salt; a few bay leaves; a whole Jamaica and black pepper; 1 quart of stale, strong beer; and a little vinegar. If you make the pickle very well, it will keep 5 or 6 months very well. If your beef is not too much baked, it will cut all diamonds.

Author's note: Please consume this within a week. I doubt our modern gut constitutions could handle beef that old. As of April 2023, the French Court of Appeals confirmed that food-watch NGO Yuka was legally legitimate in describing saltpeter a "cancer risk." Saltpeter, also known as sodium nitrate, helps kill botulism and makes meat red when cooked, and there is no known substitute.

TO POT ALL SORTS OF WILD FOWL

4 ducks, dove or quail
4 tablespoons mace
4 tablespoons nutmeg
Pepper to taste
4 tablespoons salt
4 tablespoons clarified butter or ghee

When the wild fowl are dressed, take a rolling pin and beat them on the breast until flat. Before you roast them, season them with mace, nutmeg, pepper and salt. You must not roast them over much; when you draw them, season them on the outside and set them on one end to drain out the gravy. Then put them into your pot. You may put them in 2 layers if you press them very flat. Cover them with clarified butter when they are cold.

TO MAKE HAM PYE

1 small ham (bone-in)
Pepper to taste
½ pound butter
2 premade pie crusts
Puff pastry pie cover (for baking)

Cut the ham round, and lay it in water all night. Boil it tender, as you would do for eating. Take off the skin, strew over it a little pepper and bake it in a deep dish; then put to it a pint of water and a ½ pound of butter. You must bake it in puff pastry, but lay no pastry in the bottom of the dish. When you send it to the table, send it without a lid. This is proper for a top or bottom dish in either summer or winter.

TO MAKE A HAUNCH OF VENISON

1 venison leg
Premade pizza dough ball
Premade sweet sauce (like Branston Pickle)

Take a haunch of venison and spit it. Then take a little bread meal, knead it and roll it very thin. Lay it over the fat part of your venison with a paper over it; then tie it around your venison with a pack thread. If it is a large haunch, it will take 4 hours of roasting; a middling haunch will take 3 hours. Keep it basting while you roast it. When you dish it up, put a little gravy in the dish and sweet sauce in a bason. Half an hour before you draw your venison, take it off the paste, baste it and let it be a light brown.

TO MAKE AN OYSTERS PYE

1 pint large oysters
1 loin veal, sliced and seasoned with salt and pepper
Marrow of 2 beef bones
Premade pie pastry (for cover)
2 tablespoons white wine

Oysters pye.
Author's collection.

Take 1 pint of the largest oysters you can get, and clean them very well in their own liquor (or water). Take the kidney or loin of veal, cut it in thin slices and season it with a little pepper and salt. Lay the slices in the bottom of the dish without pastry on the bottom. Cover them with the oysters and strew over a little bit of the seasoning you did for the veal; then take the marrow of two bones, lay it over your oysters and cover them with puff paste. When it is baked, take off the lid, put into it a spoonful or two of white wine, shake it up all together and serve it up. This is proper for a side dish at either noon or night.

TO MAKE AN ORANGE PYE

6 Seville oranges (or other large orange variety)
6 to 8 apples
½ pound powdered sugar
Additional ¾ pound powdered sugar
Puff pastry (for pie topper)

Take 6 Seville oranges and chip them very fine, as you would do for preserving. Make a hole in the top and scoop out all the meat, as you would do an apple. You must boil them while they are tender, and shift them 2 or 3 times to take off the bitter taste. Take 6 or 8 apples, pare and slice them and put to them part of the pulp of your oranges, picking out the strings and pippins. Put to them a ½ pound of fine powder sugar, so boil it up over a slow fire, as you would do for puffs, and fill out oranges with it. They must be baked in a deep Delft dish with no pastry underneath them. When you put them into your dish, put under them ¾ of a pound of fine powder sugar; put in as much water as you need to wet your sugar and place your oranges with the open side on top. It will take about 1½ hour baking in a slow oven. Lie over them a light puff paste; when you dish it up, take off the lid and turn the oranges in the pie, then cut the lid in snippets and set them at an equal distance. Serve it up.

TO MAKE RICE PANCAKES

½ pound white rice
1 pint heavy cream
4 egg yolks
Pinch nutmeg and salt
½ pound butter
Flour for roux

Take a ½ pound of rice, wash and pick it clean, and soak it for a few hours until it reaches a jelly-like consistency. When it is cold, take 1 pint of cream and the yolks of 4 eggs, beat them well together and put them to the rice with grated nutmeg and some salt. Put in a ½ pound of butter and as much flour as you need to make it thick enough to fry with as little butter as you can.

BEEFSTEAK AND OYSTER SAUCE

1 pint oysters, drained
Pinch mace
2 strips lemon peel
¼ cup cream
1 tablespoon butter
Flour to make gravy

Strain off the liquor from the oysters. Throw them in cold water to clean while simmering the liquor with a bit of mace and lemon peel. Put the oysters in and stew for a few minutes. Add a little cream and some butter rubbed in a little bit of flour. Let them boil up. Season and broil rump steaks until they are done. Add oyster sauce over the top when you are ready to serve them.

HARD SAUCE

⅓ cup butter
Cream
1 cup confectioners sugar
1 teaspoon vanilla
1 teaspoon rum

Mix softened butter, cream, sugar, vanilla and rum. Serve cold on plum dessert puddings.

POUND CAKE

1 pound butter
1 pound sifted flour
10 eggs, separated
1 teaspoon vanilla extract
2 teaspoons rum
1 pound sugar

Cream softened butter, work in flour until mixture is mealy.

Separately, beat egg yolks, vanilla, rum and sugar until it is fluffy. Add to first mixture slowly, all while beating thoroughly.

Again separately, beat egg whites until they form peaks. Add beaten egg whites to mixture and beat for 15 minutes. Pour into 2 greased loaf pans. Bake on a low heat for 1 ¼ hours.

TOFFEE DESSERT

½ cup butter
1 cup powdered sugar
1 teaspoon vanilla extract
3 eggs, separated
2 squares chocolate, melted
2 cups breadcrumbs
1 cup chopped pecans

Cream butter, sugar, vanilla, egg yolks and melted chocolate. Separately beat egg whites until they form peaks and add to mixture. Mix breadcrumbs and nuts in a separate bowl. Pour half of the crumb/nut mixture in an 8-inch square pan. Pour in chocolate mixture and top with the second half of the crumb mixture. Chill overnight.

A GULF COAST RECIPE FOR CHICKEN CURREE

This recipe was first printed in 1768. In 1811, it was published in Philadelphia as part of an essay on diseases incidental to Europeans in hot climates, along with the method of preventing their fatal consequences. I like the last sentence of the recipe, as a good, spicy curry will definitely do this to you.

2 chickens
2 quarts water
4 ounces mutton suet or butter
Boiled white rice (for serving)

Paste

1 tablespoon turmeric
½ tablespoon powdered ginger
2 teaspoons cayenne pepper
2 teaspoons black pepper
6 grains pimento
6 grains cardamom
1 or 2 cloves garlic
12 large onions

Chicken curee, possibly the oldest known printed recipe from early Pensacola. *Author's collection.*

2 chickens will make a curree for 4 or 5 persons. The chickens, after being clean picked and washed, are cut up raw into the usual pieces of wings, legs, thighs, side bones, rump, breast and neck; the liver, gizzard and heart are also thrown in. You need 1 or 2 quarts of water to boil; 3 or 4 ounces of mutton suet or butter are thrown into the boiling water with the meat; and the following ingredients, previously prepared, are beaten into a paste in a clean mortar—1 tablespoon of turmeric, ½ tablespoon of powdered ginger, 2 teaspoonfuls of red pepper and the like quantity of black pepper, 6 grains of pimento and of cardamom, 1 or 2 cloves of garlic, and 12 large onions. All these ingredients, well beaten into a paste, are added to the meat, and the whole is boiled until the chicken is sufficiently dressed and the spices blended into the soup.

This is served up in a deep dish, with a similar dish of rice well and dry boiled. The rice is first placed on a plate, and the curree meat and soup poured over it with a spoon. The food is eaten with the spoon in the right hand, a fork in the left. Acids are used according to taste, and catsup is sometimes mixed when it is made in the soup manner. This dish may be made of any fresh meat cut up to spoon meat size, such as veal, mutton, lamb, whole eggs, tripe, shrimps, lobsters, whitefish or oysters.

This food, which gives a high relish for water as a drink, produces a most salutary effect on the whole system; the stomach is strengthened; the spirits exhilarated; the necessary evacuations are promoted without violence or excess.

CATSUP

We all know the most beloved condiment in the United States. Catsup (or ketchup) is as ubiquitous as tree leaves. However, catsup was originally made with mushrooms. Northwest Florida has only a few wild edible mushrooms, and the citizens could have made it here. But merchants were certainly able to ship mushroom catsup from outside the area to Pensacola. If you forage for the local woodear, turkeytail and lion's mane mushrooms, be absolutely certain you know what you are doing. This recipe calls for common cremini mushrooms that you can buy at any grocery store.

Catsup. Originally made with mushrooms, this is a tasty condiment that is very easy to make. *Author's collection.*

2 pounds cremini mushrooms
3 tablespoons coarse salt
2 bay leaves
1 medium white onion, chopped
Zest of 1 lemon
¼ teaspoon ground cloves
½ teaspoon allspice
1 tablespoon ground horseradish
1 pinch ground cayenne pepper
¼ to ½ cup apple cider, malt or white vinegar

Chop mushrooms and salt them, Cover and let sit for 10 minutes without disturbing. Stir mushrooms and add bay leaves. Then let sit for 8-plus hours (overnight) refrigerated in an airtight container. Add chopped onion and the rest of the ingredients to the mushroom mixture and stir until well mixed. Boil for 15 minutes. Let cool and press the liquids out of the mushrooms. Really press down to make sure you squeeze all the liquids out. Bottle and jar the liquid.

Author's note: Bring liquid to a boil and then reduce to medium. This way, the mushrooms will release their liquid without it evaporating. Save the cooked mushrooms and add to soups, stews or serve over rice to eliminate waste.

Local seafood would have been consumed at this time and was mainly baked or roasted or served in a "pye" like the oyster pie described earlier. Although raw oysters would've been consumed as well. The British prefer to eat raw oysters with vinegar, as kind of a basic mignonette, possibly with shallots or onions added. Nowadays Gulf Coast residents like a splash of cayenne hot sauce, lemon/lime juice, or a horseradish/ketchup cocktail sauce on a basic saltine cracker. I like to slurp 'em right out of the shell.

6

SPAIN AGAIN, THE CREOLES, FRENCH CHEFS

Things are going well for the citizens of Pensacola. The city is expanding, commerce is humming like an overexcited bee and the future is bright. Then on December 16, 1773, a bunch of disgruntled peasants tossed English tea into the Boston Harbor, and we all know how that turned out.

In 1776, King Charles III of Spain decided that some covert assistance to the newly declared United States could be attained without formally declaring an alliance. With the British military busy in New England, wrangling with General Washington, there was a token force of two thousand British troops in Pensacola. On March 9, 1781, Spanish General Bernardo de Gálvez attacked and captured Pensacola, expelling the British for good.

Now that Pensacola was under Spanish control again, things changed drastically. First of all, the British left, which shrunk the population down to a few hundred. Most of the businesses closed, and most of the port was now not in use. Bummer. At that time, Spain could militarily occupy Pensacola, but it couldn't govern it very efficiently, especially its economy.

The Spanish government allowed some British merchants, particularly Panton, Leslie & Co., to operate in Pensacola. Panton, Leslie & Co., were Scottish merchants who operated trade in the Bahamas and southeastern United States. They had exclusive contracts with the Native tribes and were able to move all kinds of merchandise and food into Pensacola for consumption and export.

Just to tick off the British, the Spanish allowed escaped enslaved people to live free in Northwest Florida, so they arrived when they could and added their cooking traditions to the area as well.

THE CREOLES

No other culture is more important to Pensacola's culinary traditions than the Creole. It is the dominant cooking culture in the city.

Creoles first moved into the area around the time Presidio Panzacola was built in 1754. There are a couple of things to set straight before we move forward. Creoles comprise a culture. As there were several races of people living along the Gulf Coast back then, they usually had to go along to get along. This was (and still is) a harsh area for humans to exist in. Many peoples intermarried and then intermarried again for generations, creating a unique culture that drew from many backgrounds and culinary traditions. A Creole can be any of the following: Native, African, French, Spanish, Caribbean and English (and, in New Orleans, German and Italian). Each brought in their culinary traditions and mixed them with others time and again throughout the years, making a truly unique cuisine that is famous all over the world.

Creole cooking is *not* Cajun. They are two distinct cooking styles that share some of the same recipes and ingredients, but they have different outcomes. Creoles predate the Cajuns. Creole cooking is known to be more refined "city" food, while Cajun food is rustic country food. Creole food is spicy, while Cajun food could be considered hot. The Creoles tended to live on the coast and had access to more ingredients via the shipping ports, while Cajuns relied on what they could hunt, fish and grow in the swamps, along the coasts and in the hammock forests of lower Louisiana.

Most restaurants in Pensacola offer up gumbo, red beans and rice, jambalaya, po'boy sandwiches and the like. Kids who grow up in Pensacola eat this at home all the time. It's a way of life here.

Now that's out of the way, Creoles moved in and out of Pensacola over the decades, moving in between New Orleans; Mobile, Alabama; and Pensacola. When Spain came back in 1781, the Creoles were a sizeable population in Pensacola.

FRENCH CHEFS

In 1789, the French Revolution kicked off, and it ended in 1799. The French monarchy and nobility were deposed and decapitated. What is not common knowledge is that the French chefs were also targeted because they served the elites and benefited off the backs of the poor. So, their heads were also on the chopping block. Some chefs managed to escape France, but where were they to go? The Gulf Coast was the closest French enclave where they could live without losing their heads. Although we don't know how many arrived in Pensacola, local historians claim some of them did indeed come to the city. Since Pensacola's population was rather small and available employment was scarce, most of these chefs moved on to Mobile and New Orleans, but they did leave their mark in Pensacola before moving on. New, lighter styles of cooking came with the French chefs. At that time, the cooking in the area was still heavy peasant "country" cooking, and the French brought refined sauces and new braising, sautéing, and baking techniques. Soufflés, puddings and pies made their way into the local cuisine, albeit made with what the locals could get.

THE HOLY TRINITY

Creole and Cajun cuisine relies on "the holy trinity" as the basis for most of their dishes. The holy trinity is the creole version of the French *mirepoix* (meer-pwah). Mirepoix is a blend of seasoning vegetables known as "aromatics." Diced onions, carrots and celery make up mirepoix, usually in a ratio of one part celery, two parts onion and one part carrot. It's cooked in fat, butter or oil to sweeten and deepen the flavors of a dish. It's cooked over a low heat to not caramelize the sugars, only develop the vegetables' natural flavors. It's used as the basis for soups, stews, sauces, braises and more.

The holy trinity is slightly different. Carrots do not grow well along the Gulf Coast, particularly in the sandy, acidic soil around Pensacola and the moist, swampy soil around New Orleans. The Creoles substituted the green bell pepper for carrots. This changes much of the flavor of the mirepoix, because bell peppers have a more "peppery" flavor (for lack of a better term) and much less natural sugar than carrots. The mirepoix's ratios apply to the holy trinity, but it depends on the individual. If you want more celery or bell pepper, add it. You do you. When garlic is added to the mix, it's known as the "holy trinity with the pope."

The Creoles and Cajuns put the holy trinity in darn near everything. If you make Creole food often, it can be beneficial to chop up a larger amount of these vegetables and store it in an airtight container in your fridge. It can keep for up to a week that way. Our local Publix carries pre-chopped holy trinity in its produce section.

GAZPACHEE

Gazpachee is a dish unique to Pensacola that came about in the early 1800s. We've all heard of the Spanish cold tomato soup gazpacho. Gazpachee is a play on that. At heart, gazpachee is a panzanella (Spanish bread salad). This is a dish made with gazpacho soup and hardtack. The hardtack crackers soak up the liquid from the soup, making this a spongey, tangy dish that is enjoyed in Pensacola during the peak summer tomato season.

2 hardtacks (can substitute older/dried baguettes)
2 large tomatoes
2 cucumbers
1 large sweet pepper
1 onion, chopped
3 hard-boiled eggs
Dash of vinegar

Soak hardtack for 15 minutes and squeeze out liquid. Cut tomatoes into bite-size chunks, and cut cucumbers and sweet pepper into thin slices. Slice onion into thin rings. Grate eggs. Place in a bowl in layers with hardtack on the bottom and top. Add vinegar to the vegetables in the process. Let sit for 20 minutes before serving.

JAMBALAYA

Next to gumbo, jambalaya is the most famous dish in Creole cookery. It's a staple in restaurants and homes all over the Gulf Coast, from Texas to Tampa. Jambalaya is a rice dish that has Spanish origins. Essentially, jambalaya is

Gazpachee originated in Pensacola. It's a combination of gazpacho, a cold tomato soup and a panzanella, a Spanish bread salad. *Author's collection.*

Jambalaya, a dish that came about from paella. Due to a lack of saffron, tomatoes were used to color the dish red. *Author's collection.*

paella. Paella is made with saffron, which is expensive and costly to produce, harvest and ship, especially overseas. The Spanish had to make do with what was available on the Gulf Coast, so they used tomatoes. The Creoles took it further by adding the holy trinity and chili peppers. Paella morphed into jambalaya over time.

Jambalaya can and is made with many different meats, and there are even some modern vegetarian/vegan options out there as well.

Nowadays, there are ready-made ingredient mixes in boxes and bags available at grocery stores, Zatarain's being the most recognizable brand that sells Creole/Cajun food. The following recipes originated in New Orleans in the 1800s, taken from *The Picayune's Creole Cookbook*.

CREOLE JAMBALAYA

1 pound fresh pork
2 onions
2 cloves garlic
2 sprigs thyme
2 sprigs parsley
2 bay leaves
2 cloves, ground very fine
2 tablespoons butter
1 slice ham, chopped
12 fine pork sausages
2 quarts beef broth or hot water
1½ cups rice
Salt, pepper and cayenne to taste

Cut the pork (very fine, lean and fat) into pieces about half an inch square. Chop the onions very fine and mince the garlic and thyme and parsley. Add whole bay leaves. Grind the cloves. Put 2 tablespoons of butter into a saucepan and add the onions and pork to let them brown slowly. Stir frequently and let them continue browning. When lightly browned, add the chopped ham and the cloves of garlic. Then add the herbs—thyme, bay leaves, parsley and cloves. Let all this brown 5 minutes longer and add the 12 fine sausages, cut apart, and let all cook 5 minutes longer. Then add the beef broth and let it cook for 10 minutes. When it comes to a boil, add the rice and half a teaspoon of salt and pepper to taste. The Creoles heavily season with cayenne. Let all boil 30 minutes longer or until the rice is firm. Stir often to mix well and serve.

SHRIMP JAMBALAYA

2 onions
3 ribs celery
1 bell pepper
2 tablespoons butter
1 tablespoon flour
2 sprigs thyme
1 bay leaf
2 sprigs parsley
2 cloves garlic
½ teaspoon cayenne pepper
3 large tomatoes
3 quarts broth, or oyster liquor
80 shrimp
1½ cups rice
Salt, pepper and cayenne to taste

Chop onions, celery and bell pepper very fine and put into a saucepan to brown with 2 tablespoons of butter. After a few minutes, add 1 tablespoon of flour and stir well. Then add chopped thyme, bay leaf and parsley and 2 cloves of garlic, minced very fine. Let all of this fry for 5 minutes, stirring vigorously so as not to burn the mixture. Add ½ teaspoon of cayenne pepper and 3 large tomatoes, chopped fine, and also add their juice. Let simmer for 10 minutes longer. Then add 3 quarts of broth, or water—or if it's Friday and you don't eat meat, add oyster liquor that has been heated to boiling point. Let boil and then add shrimp, rice, salt, pepper and cayenne pepper to taste. Then let boil for 30 minutes longer, or until rice is cooked, stirring occasionally. Serve hot.

Author's note: I don't recommend adding shrimp until 5 minutes before serving. Adding shrimp too early overcooks it and makes the shrimp tough and rubbery.

FIG PUDDING

3 cups ripe figs
1 cup sugar
1 teaspoon melted butter
⅓ cup flour
1 teaspoon nutmeg

Mash figs into a paste and add sugar, butter, flour and nutmeg. Pour into a square pan. Bake at 250 degrees until browned.

SPANISH RICE SALAD

2 cups cooked rice
4 tomatoes, peeled and cubed
2 green peppers, finely sliced
½ chopped onion
¾ cup olive oil
¼ cup wine vinegar
Salt and pepper to taste
1 clove garlic, minced
2 sliced hard-boiled eggs

Mix rice, tomatoes, peppers and onion. In a bowl, vigorously mix oil, vinegar, salt, pepper and garlic. Add to rice mixture and mix well. Let stand for 1 hour before serving. The Spanish like to garnish this dish with sliced olives and sliced hard-boiled eggs.

CALAS (RICE FRITTER)

1 cake compressed yeast
2 tablespoons water
1 cup cooked rice
½ cup sugar
½ cup flour
½ teaspoon salt
1 teaspoon nutmeg
3 eggs

Oil for deep frying
Powdered sugar for garnish

The night before, dissolve yeast into 2 tablespoons warm water. Then add to rice and place somewhere warm overnight. The next day, beat sugar, flour, salt and nutmeg into rice. Cover and let sit for 15 minutes. Heat oil and drop rice batter in tablespoon-size pieces at a time. Fry until lightly brown on both sides. Sprinkle with powdered sugar.

CREOLE BORDELAISE SAUCE

3 tablespoons olive oil
4 cloves garlic, chopped
1 sprig fresh thyme
1 bay leaf
2 tablespoons fresh lemon juice
½ stick (4 tablespoons) unsalted butter, cubed
1 teaspoon chopped parsley
Salt and pepper to taste

Add oil to heated saucepan. Add garlic, thyme and bay leaf. Sauté while stirring until garlic is lightly browned (do not burn). Add lemon juice and cold cubed butter and stir until melted. Strain sauce through a fine sieve and add back to pan. Add parsley, salt and pepper to taste.

BASIC CREOLE SAUCE

12 tomatoes
1 pint water
Salt and pepper to taste
1 tablespoon butter
1 sprig thyme, minced fine
1 sprig parsley, minced fine
2 bay leaves
2 garlic cloves
6 shallots
1 sweet pepper, chopped
1 tablespoon flour
Small glassful of sherry

Blanch tomatoes in hot water for 20 seconds. Remove, let cool, peel and chop.

In a pot with 1 pint of water, add tomatoes, salt, pepper and butter. Bring to a boil and let cook for 10 minutes. Add minced thyme, parsley, bay leaves, garlic and simmer for 20 minutes, stirring occasionally. Remove mix from heat, mash up and strain through a sieve. Add butter to pan and sauté shallots and sweet pepper until browned. Add flour and sherry and simmer for 20 minutes, or until reduced to the desired consistency.

TABASCO SAUCE

This is the most famous of the Creole sauces, made from the celebrated Louisiana tabasco pepper. This recipe was used in all the old Creole homes along the Gulf Coast. Note: Tabasco is a trademarked name of the same sauce created in 1868 by Edmund McIlhenny and named after the actual tabasco pepper. You can still make the sauce and not infringe on the trademark—as long as you don't sell it under that particular name. Actually, most Creole/Cajun hot sauces are made this way.

3 dozen tabasco or cayenne peppers
1 clove garlic
¼ pint spiced vinegar

Chop peppers and garlic very fine. Scald (sauté on high heat) until very tender. Mash mixture and press through a sieve (or blender). Add vinegar until it reaches the consistency of a rich cream. Bottle and seal.

CREOLE MUSTARD

1 pint white wine
1 teaspoon ground celery seed
1 teaspoon ground cloves
1 teaspoon ground allspice
1 teaspoon ground mace
1 clove garlic
1 teaspoon salt
1 pound ground brown mustard seeds
Tarragon vinegar
Cider

Pour a pint of wine in a saucepan, add mixed spices (apart from mustard seeds), garlic and salt. Steep on a medium-low heat for 1 hour. Mix ground mustard seeds into the wine with equal parts tarragon vinegar and cider. Make into a paste while boiling hot. Let cool and jar.

SWEET POTATO BREAD

1 pint milk
½ cake compressed yeast
1 teaspoon salt
2 tablespoons butter
1½ pints flour, sifted
1 quart smashed baked sweet potatoes

Combine milk, yeast, salt and melted butter into a bowl, beat thoroughly and set overnight in a warm place. The next day, add sifted flour to mashed sweet potatoes and then combine with yeast mixture. Beat into a light sponge batter, cover and set aside to rise in a warm place until it doubles in size. Turn out on a bread board and mold into loaves. Set on a greased pan and bake in a moderately warm oven for 45 minutes.

COLLARDS

Nothing screams Southern cooking more than collard greens. A staple in houses all over the South, collards are to Southerners what rice is to people in Asia. Collards date back thousands of years and originated in the areas around ancient Greece. Collards are the oldest leafy green in the cabbage family and were cultivated and eaten all over Europe. Collards arrived with enslaved Africans in Jamestown in the 1600s. At the time, collards were typically boiled in a pot with salted meat. Over the years, people "doctored them up" with aromatic vegetables, like onions, and used meat broth and other seasonings. You may even buy packets of collard seasonings at local grocery stores. Collards are usually eaten with a few healthy dashes of pepper vinegar, and the "pot likker" is sopped up with a big slab of cornbread.

Collards, as common as sand on the Gulf Coast. *Author's collection.*

SIMPLE COLLARD GREENS

2 bunches fresh collards
Water or meat broth
4 ounces of any of the following: salt pork, smoked ham, tasso ham, smoked pork jowls, ham bone, smoked turkey leg
½ onion, diced
Red pepper flakes to taste

Rinse greens several times under cold running water to remove dirt. Tear leaves from stems and slice collards into ½-inch strips (or chop into large squares). Bring water or broth to a boil. Add onions, chopped meat and collards. Boil for 10 minutes and reduce to a simmer. Simmer for 30 minutes for firm greens, 45 minutes if you prefer them softer. Serve in a bowl—meat/onions and all—add pepper flakes to taste, sop up pot likker with cornbread.

BAKED GRITS

Grits are another staple that are uniquely Southern in nature. Dry corn is ground in a mill to produce a rough cornmeal. There is evidence that cornmeal was being ground and eaten with heated water as early as 8,700 BCE in Central America. The introduction of grits to Europeans in the New World came from the Muskogee Natives. The consumption of grits was adopted by the settlers and spread throughout the South. Once considered a poor person's food, grits have now been elevated to gourmet status. Shrimp and grits are on every other restaurant's menu all over Pensacola. Smoked Gouda cheese, stewed tomatoes and sausage have been added to make grits a very versatile dish, all the while retaining its deep Southern roots.

1 cup dry grits
½ quart milk
½ quart water
Salt and pepper to taste
2 eggs, separated
4 ounces heavy cream

Preheat oven to 350 degrees. Boil the grits in a milk-water mixture. Season with salt and pepper. When quite dry, take off the stove and let cool a little. Beat egg whites and the yolks of two eggs separately. When grits are cool, add the yolks and blend thoroughly. Do the same for the whites and add cream. Place in oven and bake until grits are a beautiful brown color. Serve hot.

RED BEANS AND RICE

Red beans and rice make what is arguably the most popular Creole dish next to gumbo and jambalaya. It originated in New Orleans as a dish made on Mondays. Monday was laundry day in New Orleans for housewives, professional laundresses, hotels, etc. Laundry was an all-day event, and "NOLA" ladies needed to make a dinner that didn't require much in the way of preparation or cooking. The dish of red beans and rice was born out of necessity. Dried red beans could be placed in a pot with Sunday's leftover ham bone. The beans could simmer all day, requiring little to no attention. Eventually, the dried beans would be broken down into a thick, rich gravy. Rice was always kept in the house, so the red bean mix could be ladled over a bowl of rice and served to the family. If you ever get red beans and rice at a restaurant and there's no thick gravy, it may taste good, but it ain't a proper plate of red beans and rice.

1 quart dried red beans
1 pound ham or salted meat, diced
1 sprig thyme
1 bay leaf
1 onion, finely minced
1 bell pepper, finely minced
2 stalks celery, finely minced
Salt and pepper

Wash the beans and put in a pot of cold water, enough to cover the beans by 3 inches. Let the water heat slowly and add meat, herbs and vegetables. Bring to a boil, reduce to a low simmer and let cook for several hours, stirring every once in a while. When beans are tender, mash some with a potato masher in the pot. Ladle over cooked rice, add hot sauce if desired and serve.

LIMA BEANS CREOLE STYLE

Lima beans arrived in the United States with enslaved Africans. They are not native to North America. Lima beans are one of the most widely grown and consumed legumes in the United States. While they are traditionally boiled with some onions and seasonings, the Creoles put their own spin on them.

3 pints water
1 pint fresh baby lima beans (if frozen beans, thawed)
1 teaspoon salt
½ pint heavy cream (or milk)
1 tablespoon flour
1 tablespoon butter

Salt and pepper to taste
1 sprig thyme
1 sprig parsley
1 bay leaf

Bring 3 pints of water to a boil and add beans. Boil until tender, about 2 hours. After they have boiled for 1 hour, add 1 teaspoon of salt. Then drain water and return beans to pot. Add ½ a pint of cream or milk, 1 tablespoon of flour blended well with butter, salt and pepper to taste, 1 sprig of thyme, 1 sprig of parsley and 1 bay leaf, minced very fine. Let simmer for 10 minutes and serve hot.

GUMBO

Gumbo is the quintessential Creole and Cajun dish. Gumbo recipes vary from region to region, cook to cook. Gumbo's origins are shrouded in mystery, but food scholars all agree it originated in southern Louisiana and has ingredients derived from the area's diverse population—Native, African, French, Caribbean, Spanish and German (sausages). Author C. Paige Gutierrez wrote in her book *Cajun Foodways*, "Gumbo is an economical dish, useful for feeding a large number of people with a small amount of meat or seafood."

Food historians agree that gumbos were originally used as a way to feed a lot of people with a small amount of food. Usually, small amounts of meat and seafood could be stretched by adding them to a soup and ladling them over a bowl of rice. Nowadays, gumbo has been raised to an art form, and gumbo competitions occur all over the Southeast, especially along the Gulf Coast.

Gumbo most likely took its name from okra. Okra arrived in the new world with enslaved Africans. The West Africans called the vegetable *gombo* or *combo*. There are other conflicting bits of info on the dish's name, but this makes the most sense to most people. Not all gumbos contain okra, but the vegetable is used as a thickener as well as a flavoring agent.

Gumbo is always made with a roux (ROO). Roux is made by mixing flour and fat over a high heat, preferably in a cast iron skillet. Roux is a thickening agent used in soups, sauces and stews. It also adds a nutty flavor to the dishes.

Roux can vary in color from a light tan to a dark and brooding brown. The darker the roux, the more intense the flavor. Some cooks add roux in the beginning of the cooking process, while sautéing the holy trinity, and some add it later, after the broth is introduced to the soup.

Though gumbo has humble origins, it has been elevated to an art form in modern times. Famous chefs like Emeril Lagasse, Thomas Keller and the father of haute French cuisine, Auguste Escoffier, have their own recipes for the dish. Gumbo cookoffs are monstrously popular along the Gulf Coast, where professional chefs, restaurateur and aspiring home cooks labor lovingly over pots of gumbo, hoping to take home the blue ribbon.

Author's note: Creole gumbo is not Cajun gumbo. They share some ingredients and techniques but are made and taste differently. Cajuns do not have an influence on historical Pensacola cuisine, so they will not be included here. Creole gumbo is thickened with okra. Cajun gumbo is thickened with filé (FEE-LAY, powdered sassafras leaves). The Cajuns borrowed the ingredient from Natives, who also used it to thicken their stews. You do not *use both okra and filé to thicken soups in polite society. Otherwise, you will not be invited to join the Junior League. However, many home cooks and restaurants may have a jar of filé on the table to add a sprinkle or two to your bowl merely as a flavor-enhancer.*

RECIPE FOR A BASIC ROUX

Any fat may be used—oil, lard, duck fat, bacon grease, etc. Depending on the gumbo I cook, I use a different fat.

¾ cup vegetable oil
1 cup flour

Heat skillet and add oil. Gradually mix in flour and stir constantly so the flour won't burn. The heat should be medium-high. It takes time to make a roux—up to and beyond 30 minutes. Depending on how you like your flavor, you may stop cooking roux when it's a little darker than cardboard or as dark as a good coffee. Remove from heat and let cool. This is enough for five quarts of gumbo. Roux can last for several weeks in an airtight container in the refrigerator. I like to make a large batch and freeze it. It will last for 6 months in a freezer. You may cut or break off chunks as you need it.

GUMBO FOUR WAYS

The most popular gumbo types are those that use seafood and chicken and sausage. Duck and andouille sausage gumbo is a popular treat, and the meat-free gumbo z'herbes are eaten widely by the Catholic population on meatless days and during Lent.

Seafood Gumbo

Seafood gumbo can contain all types of seafood, but the most common ingredients are shrimp, crab, oysters and fish. Gumbos take time to make if you start from scratch. A rich seafood broth is required for this dish. I like to make it a day ahead of time by roasting the shrimp shells; adding fish backs/sides and heads to the broth with onions, carrots, celery; and simmering it over a low heat for two-plus hours. You may use chicken broth, but it won't taste as good as a seafood broth.

½ stick (4 tablespoons) unsalted butter, cubed
2 onions, chopped
1 green bell pepper, chopped
2 stalks celery, chopped
2 cups chopped okra
4 quarts seafood or chicken broth
2 bay leaves
Creole seasoning blend to taste
Roux (should be medium brown for this dish)
2 pounds peeled shrimp
1 pint oysters with their liquor
1 cup cooked crab meat
2 filets firm white fish (snapper, flounder, etc.)
2 to 4 small cleaned but whole "gumbo crabs," halved (optional)

In a soup pot, melt cubed butter over high heat. Once butter is melted, lower heat to medium-high and add the holy trinity (onion, bell pepper and celery), along with okra, and sauté until clear. You want to make the vegetables sweat and release their natural flavors—do not brown them. When vegetables are ready, add the broth, bay leaves and creole seasoning to taste, bring to a boil and reduce to medium heat to simmer for up to 1 hour. Add roux and stir to fully dissolve. Once the roux is dissolved, let mixture simmer for 30 minutes to an hour to deepen the flavor. Stir occasionally.

Seafood cooks fast, so you want to add it near the end. Add shrimp, oysters with their liquor, crab meat, fish and gumbo crabs that have been split in half. Let simmer for 10 minutes and remove from heat. At this point, the gumbo is ready to serve over a bowl of cooked rice with chopped green onions and as much hot sauce as you can stand.

Like most soups, gumbo tastes better when it sits in the fridge overnight. Something magical happens, and the flavors meld together and intensify, making the gumbo taste ten times better the next day. So, if you have the willpower, let it rest overnight.

I rarely have that willpower myself.

Chicken and Sausage Gumbo

½ stick (4 tablespoons) unsalted butter
2 onions, chopped
1 bell pepper, chopped
2 stalks celery, chopped
2 bay leaves
2 pounds smoked sausage, any kind will do
4 quarts chicken broth
Creole seasoning
2 pounds cooked and shredded chicken (or cubed, your choice)
Roux (should be a light to medium brown for this dish)

Heat a skillet on medium-high heat and add butter. When butter is melted add onion, bell pepper, celery, bay leaves and sausage, and sauté until onions become translucent. Do not brown. When vegetables are ready, add broth and creole seasoning to taste. Bring to a boil, reduce heat, add chicken and let simmer for up to 1 hour. Add roux, stir until it's dissolved and then let simmer for up to 1 hour, stirring occasionally. Ladle over cooked rice; add filé and hot sauce to taste.

Duck and Andouille Gumbo

This dish has Cajun origins that were adopted by the Creoles. Andouille (AHN-DOO-EE) has origins in France and was eventually made in southern Louisiana by the Cajuns and Creoles alike, who used the available ingredients to make a mildly spicy smoked sausage that is most popularly used in both Cajun and Creole cooking. The roux for this dish should be very dark and bold.

Oil, tallow, lard or duck fat (preferrable)
2 duck breasts, fat scored
1 pound andouille sausage, cut into coins
1 onion, chopped
1 green bell pepper, chopped
1 rib celery, chopped
23 ounces chicken broth
Creole seasoning
Dark roux
Cooked rice
2 bay leaves
Chopped scallions
Fresh thyme

In a pot or dutch oven over medium-high heat, melt the fat or oil. Add the duck breasts, fat side down. Cook until browned, about 5 minutes, and then turn over and cook for another 5 minutes. Remove from heat and set aside to cool. Leave drippings in pot.

Add andouille to pot and cook until browned, stirring all the while. When browned, remove from pot with a slotted spoon; set on a paper towel to cool. Leave drippings in pan.

Add chopped vegetables to pan and cook until browned, about 10 minutes. While the vegetables are browning, dice the duck breasts. Add duck and andouille back to pot and cook for 3 minutes. Add chicken broth, bay leaves and Creole seasoning to taste. Bring to a boil, reduce heat and let simmer for 30 minutes, stirring occasionally. Add the roux to desired consistency, simmer for another 30 minutes. Serve in a bowl over cooked rice; garnish with chopped scallions, fresh thyme leaves.

Gumbo Z'herbes

Gumbo Z'herbes is a unique dish. Like all gumbos, it is made with a roux. It is a dish served during Lent, as it's a meatless dish. Over time, it began to be made with sausage and ham, but for this book's purposes, this is the vegetarian dish. It is made with greens, usually what is available, and can contain many kinds of vegetables. Legend says the more greens you have in the gumbo, the more new friends you will attain in the next year. The origins of this dish have West African and Caribbean influences, specifically those from Callaloo. Traditionally, the greens used are collards, mustard, turnip, beet and dandelion greens. Modern versions may use kale and Swiss chard.

Oil for sauteing
1 onion, chopped
1 green bell pepper, chopped
2 ribs celery, chopped
3 pounds assorted greens
2 bay leaves
32 ounces water or vegetable broth
Creole seasoning
Roux (color will be cook's preference; I tend to like a darker roux)
Cooked rice
1 bunch chopped scallions

Heat oil over medium-high heat, and add chopped onion, bell pepper and celery to cook for 10 minutes. Add greens and stir. The greens will reduce in size quickly. Occasionally stirring, let ingredients mix for another 10 minutes.

Add bay leaves, water or broth, creole seasoning and bring to a boil. Reduce heat and simmer for 30 minutes, stirring occasionally. Add roux to desired consistency and simmer for another hour. Serve over cooked rice; garnish with chopped scallions.

7

STARS AND STRIPES

When Spain gained control of Pensacola in 1783, American immigrants began moving into Northwest Florida. In 1810, many of them declared independence from Spain and rebelled. Napoleon Bonaparte had already invaded Spain, and the Spanish empire was weakened.

President James Madison and Congress used the rebellion to claim the region, knowing full well that Spain couldn't do a lot about it. In 1818, General Andrew Jackson seized the Spanish forts in Pensacola and St. Marks. In 1821, Secretary John Quincy Adams pressured Spain to cede East Florida and relinquish West Florida to the United States. Spain received no compensation for the secession; however, the United States did pay Spain the equivalent of $5 million in liability for the damage done by the American rebels in 1810. With the Transcontinental Treaty, in 1821, the United States and Spain defined the western limits of the Louisiana Purchase, and Spain surrendered its claims to the Pacific Northwest. In return, the United States recognized Spanish sovereignty over Texas. (We all know how that eventually turned out.)

Plaza Ferdinand is a park in downtown Pensacola that encompasses one full city block. Stately live oak and sweet magnolia trees dominate its landscape and provide a near full-canopy shade. On the north side of the park is a large, beautiful fountain that was originally a horse trough placed there by a ladies' charity organization in 1912. Historical monuments are located in the park, and four British cannons line the south side as a historical reminder of the area's military past.

The fountain in Plaza Ferdinand, downtown Pensacola. *Author's collection.*

The statue of Andrew Jackson, Plaza Ferdinand. *Author's collection.*

Plaza Ferdinand is a very important piece of real estate to not only Pensacola but also the nation as a whole. On July 17, 1821, the transfer of Florida to the United States began around 10:00 a.m., when Jackson rode to the steps of the Government House, which was located on the site of the present-day Pensacola Museum of History. There, he met Spanish Governor Don José María Callava. Together, they descended the steps and walked into Plaza Ferdinand, where they strode between lines of United States and Spanish troops. The Fourth Infantry band played "The Star-Spangled Banner," the Spanish flag was lowered to half-staff and the United States flag was raised to be level with it. Soldiers lowered the Spanish flag and raised the United States flag to full staff while the USS *Hornet*, in Pensacola Bay, fired a twenty-one-gun salute. After the ceremony, Jackson officially proclaimed the establishment of the Florida Territory, and a few days later, he set up a new territorial government on behalf of the United States. Andrew Jackson took up residence at 200 South Palafox Street, where 200 South Tap House sits today. The original house burned down in 1839, long after Jackson left the area.

Pensacola's population grew in leaps and bounds. The forests supplied abundant lumber opportunities, and sawmills sprang up all over the area. Plentiful mud and natural clay deposits provided opportunities to brick-makers to establish themselves and produce bricks to be used locally and shipped all over the country. The Port of Pensacola expanded again, bringing lots of shipping companies to the area. The cuisine of the area expanded, with American immigrants moving in and bringing their cooking traditions with them. Transportation was improving and brought in food and ingredients to grow Pensacola's culinary traditions. The fishing and oystering industries grew, and the fruits of the bay and Gulf of Mexico began to appear on local tables.

OYSTER STEW

3 large potatoes
3 carrots
4 medium onions
Water
4 dozen oysters and their liquor
4 cups milk
Salt and pepper to taste
Pat of butter

Peel and dice potatoes, carrots and onions. Add vegetables to soup pot and cover with enough water and oyster liquor to cover. Bring to a boil and let simmer until vegetables are tender. Add oysters and simmer until edges curl. Add milk and let simmer for 30 minutes or longer. Add salt and pepper to taste. Place a pat of butter in each bowl when serving.

FISH FRITTERS

1 ½ cups flour
2 teaspoons baking powder
½ teaspoon salt
½ teaspoon pepper
1 egg
⅔ cup milk
1 ½ cups flaked white fish
Oil for frying

Fish fritters. *Author's collection.*

Combine flour with baking powder, salt and pepper and any seasonings you wish. Beat an egg, add milk and mix in the flour mixture. Add in the flaked fish. Drop spoonfuls of the fish mixture into hot oil. You may deep fry this mixture or put just enough oil in a skillet to cover ⅓ of the fritters. Fry until browned and serve. Tartar or cocktail sauce pairs well with this dish.

OKRA FRITTERS

1 quart okra, sliced into rounds
2 eggs
1 cup flour
Salt and pepper to taste
Milk
Oil for frying

Rinse okra and cut into ¼-inch slices, place in a pot and cover with water, boil until okra is soft (30 minutes). Beat eggs and mix with flour, salt and pepper and enough milk to make a batter with the consistency of heavy cream. Mix okra into batter, drop in hot oil by the spoonful and fry until browned.

POTATO DUMPLINGS

4 medium-sized potatoes
2 tablespoons butter (room temperature)
1 pinch salt
½ teaspoon powdered nutmeg
1 egg
⅔ cup flour
⅓ cup melted butter
¾ cup breadcrumbs

Boil potatoes with peels in salted water until softened. Drain and place in a large mixing bowl. Mash hot potatoes with peel. Stir in butter, a little salt, and nutmeg and let cool. Blend in a beaten egg and just enough flour so the mixture is easy to mold. Shape dough into small balls and dredge in flour as you shape. Drop into hot water (medium-high heat) and cook for 8 to 10 minutes. Remove and put in a bowl with melted butter and sprinkle with breadcrumbs.

SUPPER BREAD

2 eggs, separated
½ cup sugar
2 cups sifted flour
2 teaspoons baking powder
½ teaspoon nutmeg
¾ cup milk
1 tablespoon melted butter

Beat egg yolks and add sugar, mixing well. Separately, mix flour, baking powder and nutmeg. Add dry mixture to the sugar/egg mixture and add milk; stir until blended. Add melted butter and mix well. Fold in beaten egg whites. Add to muffin tin and bake at a moderate heat until brown. Serve immediately.

THE RED SNAPPER

Pensacola was known as the red snapper capital of the world. With the addition of icehouses, red snapper from Pensacola was shipped all over the country. Much has been written on the industry—too much to include here, so the following is a brief history. Crews of pilot boats first noticed the red snapper in the bay's deeper waters around 1840. While waiting for ships to pilot, they fished to pass the time. The red snapper will quickly bite at anything if it's hungry, including bare hooks, which is how it earned its name. It's a beautiful bright red color, and it will quickly snap up baited hooks.

At first, locals caught them for home consumption. A cottage industry of "professional" fishermen began to sell them in the city. Over time, the fishery grew into a burgeoning industry, drawing lots of men from all over the world. Greeks, Italians, Nordics, Moroccans and more descended on Pensacola for work, and they brought their cooking traditions with them. Some stuck, like those of the Greeks and Italians, and some didn't (I'm looking at you, Norway). Many of these fishermen would spend all their pay

A replica of a fishing smack boat that hunted red snapper. *Museum of Industry, UWF Historic Village; author's collection.*

Saunders Fish Co., Palafox Wharf. *West Florida History Center.*

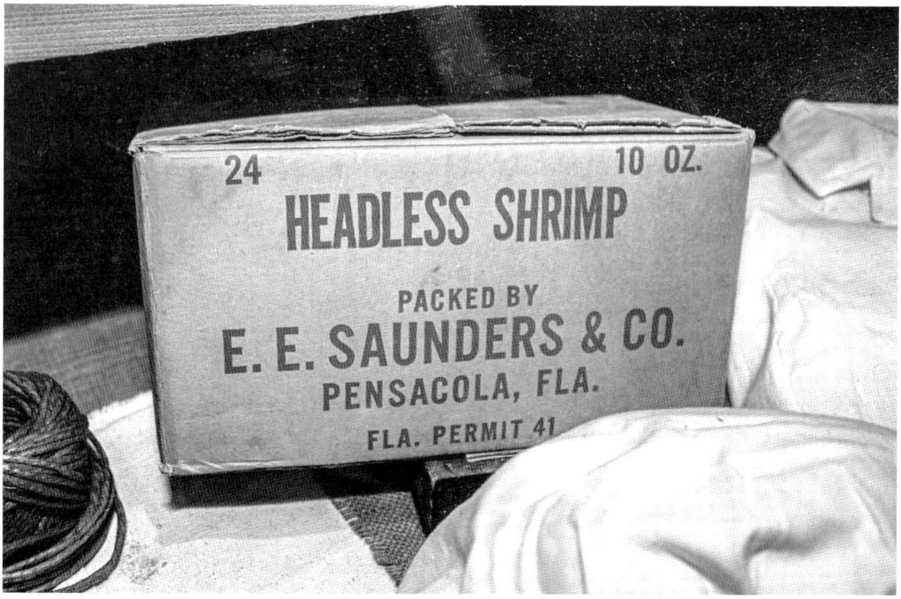

A shrimp box from Saunders Fish Co. *Museum of Industry, UWF Historic Village; author's collection.*

in the bars, taverns in downtown Pensacola—sometimes within two days. Pensacola became known as "hangover harbor." The men would quickly join outgoing fishing vessels to earn more pay. Many times, boat captains would carry passed-out drunk fishermen onto their boats, only for them to wake up already out to sea.

Several fish companies became major players, but the two largest were the Warren Fish Co. and the Saunders Fish Co. Warren owned the Baylen Street Wharf, and Saunders owned the Palafox Wharf. In 1885, the Warren Fish Co. published a small periodical/pamphlet called *The Red Snapper*. The following recipe comes directly from that publishing.

COURT BULLION

5 to 8 pounds firm white fish
2 teaspoons coloring pepper*
½ teaspoon black pepper
¼ teaspoon cayenne pepper
2 garlic cloves
½ cup lard
1 medium onion, sliced
3 tomatoes, chopped
½ cup flour

Use a fish from 5 to 8 pounds weight. Take 2 teaspoonfuls of coloring pepper, ½ teaspoon of black pepper, ¼ teaspoon of cayenne pepper, 2 teeth of garlic cut into thin slices, and put them all in a teacup and pour cold water over them. Put this in a kettle; on the fire, place ½ cup of lard, let it get very hot and slice into this a medium-sized onion and let it cook, stirring constantly. Add ½ can of tomatoes, or 3 ripe tomatoes, and let it cook well together; then put in the fish and the mixture of pepper and garlic, sufficient salt to season and ½ cup of flour. Stir well, then cover with boiling water and let it boil ten minutes. Serve at once. If your grocer does not carry coloring pepper, it can be had by addressing Warren & Co.

**Author's note: Lord knows what coloring pepper is. I searched for hours all over the internet and sent emails to food historians and came up with nothing. Coloring pepper could be multicolored peppercorns (it's probably this). But this recipe includes black pepper, so it would be "pepper heavy." It also includes cayenne pepper, which is red, so that can't be it. It may be paprika or a paprika blend—your guess is as good as mine. It could be similar to solid crab boil ingredients, like a mixture of mustard seed, coriander seed, bay leaves, dill seed and allspice.*

SYLLABUB

1 cup red wine
1 cup granulated sugar
1 quart heavy cream
1 lemon, juice and zest

Originally, syllabub was introduced to Pensacola by the British. It is a sweetened wine-based drink that includes sugar and heavy cream. Sounds kind of gross. Over time, it grew into a dessert.

The following is the original wine beverage.

In a punch bowl, add 1 cup of red wine (claret, sherry, madeira or even sangria). Stir in 1 cup of granulated sugar until it's dissolved. Beat in 1 quart of heavy cream. Stir in the juice of 1 lemon and the zest of that lemon.

PERLOO

Perloo's origins are mixed. What we do know is that pilaf and pilau are nearly similar dishes, which have origins in Europe. There is a culture on the coasts of the southeastern United States called the Gullah Geechee; the members of this culture are the descendants of enslaved Africans who lived in the Gullah corridor, from North Carolina to Jacksonville, Florida. Due to their coastal location, they developed a unique cuisine based on the available seafood, land animals and rice—lots of rice. The Gullahs brought rice with them from West Africa and are credited with being the first to bring it to the Southeast. Carlos Lavallet owned a plantation near Pensacola from 1814 to 1849. The neighborhood of Lavallet in Pensacola is named after him. Among other things, he had a rice plantation on that land, and the remains of rice ditches can be found near the old brick chimney monument in the wetlands of the area, near the lowlands connected to Escambia Bay.

Some Gullah folks did end up in Pensacola, and their descendants still cook the traditional recipes in their homes and churches.

SHRIMP PERLOO

2 tablespoons fat (lard preferred, as it's closer to the original recipe)
2 chicken breasts (or four boneless chicken thighs), cut into bite-size pieces
2 cups chopped onion
2 cloves garlic, minced
1 (14-ounce) can tomatoes, chopped (or 2 medium tomatoes, chopped)
Parsley
1 pound smoked sausage, cut into ½-inch coins
2 bay leaves
1 or 2 cayenne peppers, minced (omit if you don't like the heat;
use hot sauce to taste instead)
Cooked rice
3 cups chicken stock
2 tablespoons salt
1 pound shrimp, peeled
1 bunch scallions, chopped

Heat fat over high heat in a large pot. Add the chicken and brown on all sides. Remove and set aside. Reduce the heat to medium; add the onions, garlic, tomatoes and parsley and cook until tender, about 15 minutes, stirring frequently. Add the sausage, bay leaves and cayenne pepper (if using) and cook for about 5 more minutes. Then add the reserved chicken parts, rice and chicken stock. Add salt and mix gently.

Raise the heat and bring to a boil; then cover tightly and turn heat down very low. Cook for 45 minutes, stirring occasionally. With about 10 minutes remaining, stir in the shrimp and scallions. Then uncover and turn heat up to medium until shrimp are cooked, about 10 minutes. Spoon over a bowl of rice and add chopped scallions a garnish.

St. Francis Street Methodist Episcopal Church in Mobile, Alabama, published a cookbook in 1882 titled *Gulf City Cookbook*. Mrs. Kate Clubbs of Pensacola owned one of these books. A copy of it is in the archive in the John C. Pace Library on the campus of The University of West Florida. The following recipes are obtained from that book.

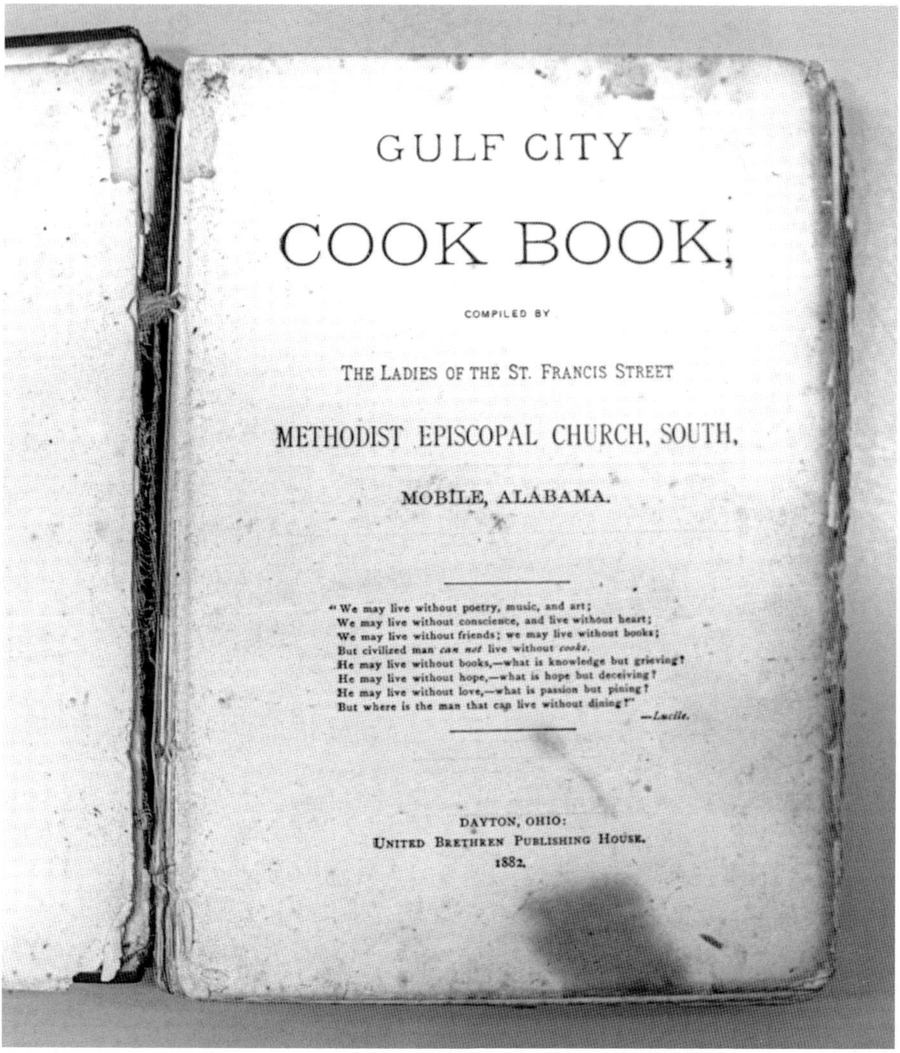

GULF CITY

COOK BOOK,

COMPILED BY

THE LADIES OF THE ST. FRANCIS STREET

METHODIST EPISCOPAL CHURCH, SOUTH,

MOBILE, ALABAMA.

"We may live without poetry, music, and art;
We may live without conscience, and live without heart;
We may live without friends; we may live without books;
But civilized man *can not* live without *cooks*.
He may live without books,—what is knowledge but grieving?
He may live without hope,—what is hope but deceiving?
He may live without love,—what is passion but pining?
But where is the man that can live without dining?"

—*Lucile*.

DAYTON, OHIO:
UNITED BRETHREN PUBLISHING HOUSE.
1882.

Above: *Gulf City Cookbook*, once owned by Ms. Kate Clubbs, a prominent Pensacola resident. *University of West Florida Archives; author's collection.*

Opposite: Interior recipes from the *Gulf City Cookbook*. *University of West Florida Archives; author's collection.*

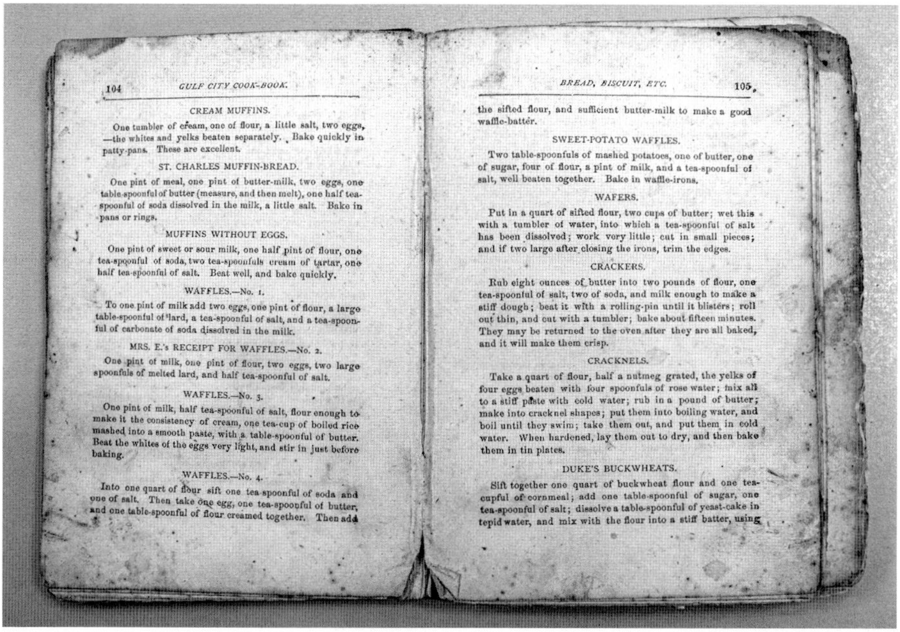

104 *GULF CITY COOK-BOOK.*

CREAM MUFFINS.

One tumbler of cream, one of flour, a little salt, two eggs, —the whites and yelks beaten separately. Bake quickly in patty-pans. These are excellent.

ST. CHARLES MUFFIN-BREAD.

One pint of meal, one pint of butter-milk, two eggs, one table-spoonful of butter (measure, and then melt), one half tea-spoonful of soda dissolved in the milk, a little salt. Bake in pans or rings.

MUFFINS WITHOUT EGGS.

One pint of sweet or sour milk, one half pint of flour, one tea-spoonful of soda, two tea-spoonfuls cream of tartar, one half tea-spoonful of salt. Beat well, and bake quickly.

WAFFLES.—No. 1.

To one pint of milk add two eggs, one pint of flour, a large table-spoonful of lard, a tea-spoonful of salt, and a tea-spoonful of carbonate of soda dissolved in the milk.

MRS. E.'s RECEIPT FOR WAFFLES.—No. 2.

One pint of milk, one pint of flour, two eggs, two large spoonfuls of melted lard, and half tea-spoonful of salt.

WAFFLES.—No. 3.

One pint of milk, half tea-spoonful of salt, flour enough to make it the consistency of cream, one tea-cup of boiled rice mashed into a smooth paste, with a table-spoonful of butter. Beat the whites of the eggs very light, and stir in just before baking.

WAFFLES.—No. 4.

Into one quart of flour sift one tea-spoonful of soda and one of salt. Then take one egg, one tea-spoonful of butter, and one table-spoonful of flour creamed together. Then add

BREAD, BISCUIT, ETC. 105

the sifted flour, and sufficient butter-milk to make a good waffle-batter.

SWEET-POTATO WAFFLES.

Two table-spoonfuls of mashed potatoes, one of butter, one of sugar, four of flour, a pint of milk, and a tea-spoonful of salt, well beaten together. Bake in waffle-irons.

WAFERS.

Put in a quart of sifted flour, two cups of butter; wet this with a tumbler of water, into which a tea-spoonful of salt has been dissolved; work very little; cut in small pieces; and if two large after closing the irons, trim the edges.

CRACKERS.

Rub eight ounces of butter into two pounds of flour, one tea-spoonful of salt, two of soda, and milk enough to make a stiff dough; beat it with a rolling-pin until it blisters; roll out thin, and cut with a tumbler; bake about fifteen minutes. They may be returned to the oven after they are all baked, and it will make them crisp.

CRACKNELS.

Take a quart of flour, half a nutmeg grated, the yelks of four eggs beaten with four spoonfuls of rose water; mix all to a stiff paste with cold water; rub in a pound of butter; make into cracknel shapes; put them into boiling water, and boil until they swim; take them out, and put them in cold water. When hardened, lay them out to dry, and then bake them in tin plates.

DUKE'S BUCKWHEATS.

Sift together one quart of buckwheat flour and one tea-cupful of cornmeal; add one table-spoonful of sugar, one tea-spoonful of salt; dissolve a table-spoonful of yeast-cake in tepid water, and mix with the flour into a stiff batter, using

OKRA SOUP

3 pounds cubed beef
3 quarts water
1 quart okra, chopped
1 pint tomatoes, chopped
1 onion, chopped fine
Salt and pepper to taste
4 hard-boiled eggs (optional)
3 to 4 ears corn, grated (optional)

Take a shank bone, or about 3 pounds of beef, and boil in 3 quarts of water until tender, skimming when necessary. Add 1 quart of chopped okra, 1 pint of prepared tomatoes, 1 onion, cut fine, and pepper and salt to taste. If desired, 4 hard-boiled eggs may be cut up and added before serving. The soup should be boiled for 3 or 4 hours. For an improvement, 3 or 4 ears of grated corn can be added.

TURTLE SOUP

1 turtle or 2 pounds prepared turtle meat
1 tablespoon lard
4 tablespoons flour
1 onion, chopped fine
1 gallon water
1 tablespoon cinnamon
1 teaspoon mace
12 to 15 whole cloves, beaten fine
1 teaspoon each thyme, parsley, salt and pepper (black and cayenne)
1 cup Madeira wine
½ cup claret or red Bordeaux

Take a turtle weighing 8 or 10 pounds, cut its head off and let it drain. Take it from its shell, select the liver and other parts being used, being careful to remove the gall. Quarter the turtle, lay it in a pan, pour boiling water over it and then scrape it clean and cut the claws off; then lay it in cold water, wash it thoroughly and wipe dry. Put into a soup kettle 1 large tablespoonful of lard and 4 of flour. Let it fry until the flour is brown; then add to it a medium-sized onion, chopped fine. Cut the meat into small pieces and fry as you would chicken, in lard and flour, for a short time. Put it all into the kettle, adding 1 gallon of water; boil slowly until it's reduced by ½. When the meat is tender, add spices as follows: 1 small tablespoonful of cinnamon, 1 teaspoonful of mace, and 12 to 15 cloves, beaten fine; also thyme, parsley, salt and pepper, both black and cayenne. Then add 1 tumbler of Madeira, and ½ tumbler of claret. If the turtle has eggs, put them in about 15 minutes before soup is served. Serve hot.

STEWED CRABS

12 blue crabs
¾ cup butter
1 large onion
10 whole cayenne peppers
2 tablespoons flour
½ pint water
2 tomatoes, chopped

Boil 12 crabs, and pick them out, being careful not to leave a particle of shell with the crabs. Take a cup about ¾ full of butter, 1 large onion, 1 pod of red pepper; fry the onion and pepper in the butter with 2 tablespoonfuls of flour, browning them nicely. Put in the crab and stir up well; add ½ pint of water and black pepper and salt to taste. Let it stew gently for 10 or 15 minutes. A couple of tomatoes, chopped, can be added to this stew as an improvement.

FISH CHOWDER, NO. 2

2 fish filets (redfish, snapper, grouper)
1½ pounds salt pork
18 Irish potatoes, sliced thin
18 tomatoes, sliced thin
6 onions, chopped fine
12 saltine crackers or 2 hardtack cakes
1 pint claret wine

Take a red or any other firm fish, cut it into pieces about 3 inches square; 1½ pounds of salt pork, cut in thin slices; 18 Irish potatoes and the same of tomatoes, both sliced thin; 6 onions, cut fine; and 12 hard crackers, broken in small pieces. Take a large pot, put a layer of pork on the bottom and then a layer each of fish, potatoes, tomatoes, onions and crackers. Sprinkle each layer with a little salt, black pepper and flour. Repeat the layers of pork, fish, potatoes, etc., until all are used. Fill with hot water until it covers the whole. Put the pot on the fire and let it boil 30 minutes; then add 1 pint of claret and boil 5 minutes longer. The chowder will then be ready for the table.

PAN HAMS

1 hog's head or cubed pork shoulder
Salt and pepper to taste
Creole seasoning to taste
2 onions chopped fine
2 teaspoons thyme
2 teaspoons sage
2 teaspoons parsley
Cornmeal (to thicken)

Take a hog's head and feet; boil them until the meat falls from the bones; withdraw them from the liquor, strain and return to the vessel. Chop the meat very fine; season with pepper, salt, spice, onions chopped fine, thyme, sage and parsley. Add all to the liquor, adding a sufficient quantity of cornmeal to make a stiff much. Let it boil 10 minutes, stirring all the time. Pour into a deep pan; when cold, cut into thin slices and fry.

SPICED BEEF

2 or more pounds beef roast
Saltpeter (sodium nitrate) to coat
2 teaspoons salt
2 teaspoons black pepper
¼ cup light brown sugar

Take a round of beef and rub it well with saltpeter; take out the bone in the middle and fill the opening with salt. Bind the round in shape or put in a bucket or some vessel that fits rather close. Let it stand for 3 days; it will make its own brine. Then take 1 spoonful of powdered spice, 1 of black pepper and 1 of brown sugar; rub the beef well with it. Then, after standing 3 days, rub it again with the spices, etc. After standing for 1 week, it will be ready for use.

Author's note: Thoroughly wash the spice mixture from beef before cooking.

HASH WITH GRAVY

1 to 2 pounds cubed stew beef
½ pint water
1 onion, diced
1 Irish potato, chopped
1 tablespoon lard
1 teaspoon flour
Salt and pepper to taste
2 teaspoons butter

Cut up your cold meat in pieces ½ inch thick; put it to stew with ½ pint of water, 1 onion, 1 Irish potato chopped fine, 1 tablespoonful of lard, 1 tablespoonful of flour, salt and pepper to taste and a little butter. Cook until the potato and onion are done; serve with the gravy.

BIRD PIE

8 doves
Prepared cornbread stuffing
Onions, chopped
1 tablespoon lard
2 teaspoons flour
1 small onion, chopped
1 pint water
24 oysters, shucked
2 tablespoons butter
Salt, pepper, allspice and nutmeg to taste
Pie pastry (for covering)

Take about 8 doves and make a stuffing of bread and onion. Stuff each bird, and then put into a stew pan about 1 tablespoon of lard and 1 dessert spoonful of flour; let it brown perfectly; cut 1 small onion very fine and fry it, adding the birds, which should fry a while before adding 1 pint of water to let boil until the birds are done. Take them out; add about 24 oysters, with a little of the oyster water, to the gravy, 1 tablespoon of butter, salt, black pepper, allspice and nutmeg; then line a baking dish with pastry, put the birds in with the gravy, and cover it over with pastry and bake.

CHICKEN FRICASSEE

1 chicken, cut into pieces
½ onion, diced
1 small piece of mace or ½ teaspoon powdered mace
Salt and pepper to taste
1 celery root (celeriac), chopped
2 egg yolks

Prepare a chicken, cut it into small pieces and put them into a saucepan with ½ an onion, a small piece of mace, salt and pepper to taste, root celery; let it boil slowly until the chicken is tender and cooked, without falling to pieces, and the water is simmered away. Just before serving, beat up the yolks of 2 eggs; pour them into the broth of the chicken, hot, and stirring well; then pour it back on the chicken, but do not let it boil or it will curdle.

BISCUITS AND GRAVY

Biscuits and gravy are about as Southern as food can get. Nothing beats a couple of fresh-baked biscuits smothered in a generous ladling of gravy for breakfast. There are even national biscuit and gravy competitions. Most Southerners use one of two gravies for their biscuits: the more-popular sausage (also known as sawmill gravy) and tomato gravy. The following are some traditional Southern recipes.

BISCUITS

Most evidence suggests that biscuits evolved from hardtack. In the South, plentiful flour, lard, pork and milk made biscuits more palatable. Yeast, although available, was expensive, and baking soda and powder were still about one hundred years away, having been introduced in the 1800s. Cooks developed a method of beating the mixture so air was trapped in the dough, giving it a bit of a rise. With the addition of baking soda and powder, coupled with modern leavening, biscuits became easier to make.

2 cups all-purpose flour
1 tablespoon baking powder
1 tablespoon granulated sugar
1 teaspoon salt
6 tablespoons unsalted butter, very cold
¾ cup whole milk or buttermilk

Preheat oven to 425 degrees and line a cookie sheet with nonstick parchment paper. Add dry ingredients to a bowl and mix well. Cut cold butter into very small pieces, add to dry ingredients and mix (with hands) until the mixture resembles very course breadcrumbs. Add milk, using a wooden spoon or spatula to stir until well mixed without overworking the dough.

Transfer your biscuit dough to a floured cutting board and use your hands to gently work the dough together. Add a bit more flour if the dough is too sticky. When the dough is firm, fold it in half over itself and use your hands to gently flatten the layers together. Rotate the dough 90 degrees and fold in half again. Repeat this 5 to 6 times. But be gentle and don't overwork the dough. Use your hands to flatten the dough to 1 inch thick and lightly dust a 2¾-inch round biscuit cutter with flour. Press the biscuit cutter straight down into the dough and drop the biscuit onto the baking sheet. Repeat until you have used as much of the dough as you can. Place biscuits less than ½ inch apart on baking sheet. Combine the remaining dough and cut out as many biscuits as you can.

Bake at 425 degrees for 12 minutes, or until the biscuits' tops are just beginning to turn a light golden brown. Brush biscuits with melted butter when done.

SAWMILL GRAVY

Sawmill, or sausage, gravy is the most popular biscuit gravy, with origins in sawmills. Lumber was a massive industry in Pensacola through the mid-1900s. Dozens upon dozens of sawmills dotted the area. Sawmill gravy was made out of necessity. Early on, biscuits were made using only flour and water. They were very dry and brittle. Pork was abundant and cheap, so a gravy made using sausage and sausage fat ladled over a biscuit made them easier to eat. It's also a very heavy, filling, calorie-dense meal that would help fuel the laboring sawmill workers.

1 pound ground pork sausage (unseasoned)
⅓ cup flour
3 to 4 cups milk
⅓ teaspoon white pepper
Salt and black pepper to taste

In a large skillet over medium heat, brown sausage, don't overcook. Add flour and stir to combine with sausage for about 2 minutes. Slowly add milk, about ½ cup at a time to prevent lumps, whisking the entire time to thicken. You may have a little milk left over, depending on how thick you like your gravy. When ready, add white pepper, salt and black pepper to taste. Serve immediately.

TOMATO GRAVY

Tomato gravy came about among poorer people. It was made to stretch ingredients on a tight budget, when tomatoes were plentiful but money was not. Tomato gravy is very versatile; many people put it over pork chops, rice and even grits (try this over Gouda shrimp and grits). Originally, this would have been made using water, but it's much more flavorful with chicken broth.

6 tablespoons bacon grease or other fat
6 tablespoons flour
1 (14½-ounce) can diced tomatoes
Salt and pepper to taste
3 cups chicken broth

Biscuits and tomato gravy. When money was scarce and tomatoes were not. *Author's collection.*

Over a medium-high heat, add fat and get it hot. Add flour and stir constantly until slightly browned. Add tomatoes and stir until heated through. Add salt and pepper. Add chicken broth and stir until mixture is thickened. If it's not thick enough, make a slurry using 2 tablespoons of flour or cornstarch mixed into cold water. Add to gravy slowly while stirring to reach desired thickness. Serve hot.

PERSIMMON PUDDING

We've discussed how terrible the soil is around the Pensacola area and how growing vegetables here is very difficult without ample fertilizing and composting—or raised beds. However, some things thrive in the area's soil. Blueberries, dewberries, muscadines, scuppernong grapes and persimmons naturally grew wild here. Locals would have made this dessert back in the day.

2½ cups granulated sugar
2 cups persimmon pulp
2 large eggs, beaten
½ teaspoon baking soda
2 cups all-purpose flour
2 teaspoons baking powder
½ teaspoon ground cinnamon
¼ teaspoon vanilla extract
½ teaspoon allspice
½ teaspoon nutmeg
1 pinch salt
2½ cups milk
4 tablespoons melted butter

Preheat the oven to 325 degrees. Grease a 9 x 13 baking dish. Combine sugar, persimmon pulp, eggs and baking soda in a mixing bowl combine until mixed well. Add flour, baking powder, cinnamon, vanilla, allspice, nutmeg and salt. Pour in milk and melted butter. Stir until mixed well. Pour into the baking pan and bake in the preheated oven for 55 minutes. You will notice the pudding rise in the oven, but it will fall when removed; this is what it is meant to do. Serve hot with whipped cream.

PERSIMMON PULP

2 pounds ripe persimmons

Peel 2 pounds of ripe persimmons, or you may scoop out the meat with a spoon. Cut the meat into ½-inch cubes, removing any seeds. Place everything in a food processor or high-speed blender. Pulse to break the fruit down, and then blend on medium-high speed until the mixture is smooth.

8

TWENTIETH CENTURY, PART I

And now we come to the time when cooking was modernized. At no time in human history have technological advances been made in such a short amount of time as they were in the twentieth century. Tall ships were still in service at the beginning of the century, and by the end, there were powerful computers that could be carried around in pockets with the whole world's knowledge available at any time.

Humans went from cooking on wood-fired cast iron stoves to using gas/electric stoves, slow cookers, pressure cookers, TV dinners, Tang (the drink of astronauts), Ron Popeil's "set it and forget it" tabletop rotisserie, air fryers—I could go on. Transportation became so advanced that food was moved all over the world. No longer were people bound to eating seasonally or locally available foods (more's the pity). You can now buy fruits and vegetables out of season. Flash-freezing allowed the nutritional value in raw foods to keep for great lengths of time. With the invention of the internet, you are now able to buy food and spices from all over the world and have them shipped right to your door.

Printing became a massive industry, and with that came an abundance of cookbooks. Churches and social and charitable organizations regularly publish cookbooks to raise money. In Pensacola, one of the most notable cookbooks is *Some Like It South*, published by the Junior League. Originally published in 1984, it is arguably the quintessential local cookbook. I'll bet more than half of the kitchens in Pensacola have it. If you don't possess it, you may have your "local card" revoked.

Garden Street looking west, downtown Pensacola. *West Florida History Center.*

Another massively popular cookbook is/was *The North Hill Cookbook*. North Hill is an affluent neighborhood located on Gage Hill (now North Hill), just on the northern edge of downtown Pensacola. Stately mansions that date to the Victorian, Edwardian and antebellum eras, as well as more early to mid-twentieth-century homes compose most of the neighborhood. It is recognized in the National Registry of Historic Places. In 1981, the North Hill Preservations Society published a compilation of recipes from North Hill residents. It was a massive seller in its day. It is now out of print but may be found online. I bought my copy on Amazon for thirty dollars.

Much needs to be said about the influence of Black Americans on Southern cooking. Enslaved Africans were the backbone of kitchens in the 1700s. They cooked in the kitchens of "the big houses" and in their slave quarters. Many had gardens around their slave quarters on plantations and grew much of their own food, and some even fished and foraged. They gained exceptional skills while working not only in the house kitchens but also in the slave quarters. They didn't have access to the ingredients they had in the big houses, so they had to get creative to make flavorful dishes using what was available to them. Their cuisine eventually became known as soul food, but it all has its influences in Southern cuisine. Okra, black-eyed peas, lima beans, sorghum and watermelons were all West African foods that arrived in

The Child Restaurant. Once a highlight of dining on Palafox Street, it was a coffeehouse in the 1800s and is now a popular dive bar. *West Florida History Center.*

Interior of The Child Restaurant. *University of West Florida Archives; author's collection.*

the New World with the slave trade, and it is to these enslaved people that we owe infinite gratitude for shaping the South's culinary heritage.

Beginning in the 1800s, fishermen from many countries descended on Pensacola to take up work in the booming snapper industry. Greeks, Italians, Nordics and more moved here and added their culinary traditions to Pensacola. Many are multigenerational restaurant owners who still own multiple restaurants in the area.

Since cooking changed so radically in such a short period, we will break this century down into two parts, beginning with the years between 1900 and 1950.

EARLY TO MID-TWENTIETH CENTURY

BREAKFAST FRITTERS (FROM *MILTON COOKBOOK*, 1906)

3 eggs, beaten
Pinch salt
1 cup sweet milk (fresh)
Baking powder
Flour
Lard (for frying)

You will need 3 eggs well beaten, a pinch of salt and 1 cup of sweet milk. Sift baking powder in flour and make a stiff batter. Drop 1 teaspoonful in a deep kettle of hot lard and fry to a nice brown. This is delicious and easily prepared for a hot breakfast.

STEWED CHICKEN ITALIAN STYLE (MRS. E. ROSASCO, *MILTON COOKBOOK*, 1906)

1 tablespoon butter
1 tablespoon olive oil
1 onion, chopped fine
1 chicken, prepared in pieces
1 (14-ounce) can diced tomatoes
Parsley, chopped (for garnish)
Salt and pepper to taste

Put in a saucepan 1 large spoonful of butter, 1 spoonful of olive oil and 1 onion chopped fine. Let this fry a little while (don't let the onion brown), and then add 1 chicken, well cleaned and cut up. Let it cook about 10 minutes, and then add some tomatoes, chopped, and some pepper. Let this cook again very slow, about 20 minutes, and a few minutes before taking it from the stove, add a little parsley, chopped very fine. This dish may be served with mashed potatoes or sweet corn.

In 1900, the Ladies' Aid Society of the Presbyterian Church of Pensacola compiled a cookbook titled *Pensacola Souvenir Cookbook*. The following recipes are from that book.

SOUP OF STUFFED LETTUCE (MRS. J.W. FRATER)

1 calf's brain, boiled with bacon
2 tablespoons chopped garlic
1 bunch parsley, chopped
½ cup grated Parmesan cheese
1 egg
Salt and pepper to taste
8 heads lettuce (iceberg)
1 box beef broth

Take 1 brain which has been boiled with a small piece of bacon and chop both; add a little garlic and parsley well chopped, a little Parmesan cheese grated, 1 egg, salt and pepper. Stir together. Take 8 heads of lettuce which have been scalded and drained, open them and put in the center a spoonful of the stuffing, close the leaves, put in a saucepan with broth to barely cover them. Cook slowly for 3 or 4 hours on top of the stove, and cover while cooking. When almost dry, add some meat gravy and serve with thin slices of toast and grated cheese.

Author's note: Unless you want to use actual brains, substitute this ingredient with ground pork.

POMPANO (PENSACOLA FISH CO. RECIPE)

4 Pompano
Salt to taste
4 pats butter
Lemon, sliced

Split fish down the back, through the head, and dry with a cloth. Then broil over a clear fire, but be careful not to burn. Salt only after the first side is cooked and turned up; dress with a little good butter and ¼ of a good lemon dropped on the flanks and center. When hot, it will permeate and develop its unsurpassed nutty flavor.

STEWED FISH

1 (14-ounce) can diced tomatoes
1 large onion
4 tablespoons chopped garlic
Salt and pepper to taste
Parsley
1 tablespoon lard or butter
2 pounds firm white fish, snapper or grouper

You will need 1 can of tomatoes, 1 large onion, a little garlic, plenty of salt and pepper, parsley chopped fine and 1 large spoonful of lard. Drop in your onions, fry very little, and then add your garlic, next your tomatoes. Cook until your tomatoes are good and done. Put in your fish, which is nicely sliced and salted and peppered, cover and cook over a very slow fire. If necessary, put in a very little water. If care is taken in cooking, no water will be needed.

GREEN TOMATO PICKLES (MRS. JOHN MCHENRY)

25 pounds green tomatoes
12 white onions
12 bell peppers
1 pint salt
1 gallon apple cider vinegar
2 pounds sugar
2 tablespoons each allspice, cloves, cinnamon and black and cayenne pepper
½ cup each ground mustard powder, turmeric and horseradish
2 tablespoons celery seed

You will need ½ bushel of tomatoes, 12 onions and 12 green peppers. Slice thin or chop fine; sprinkle over them 1 pint of salt and let stand overnight. The next morning, pour off the juice, cover with good cider vinegar and boil for 1 hour. Next, press all the juice out and pack in a jar. Add 2 pounds of sugar, 2 tablespoonfuls each of allspice, cloves, pepper and cinnamon, 1 teacupful of ground mustard, turmeric and horseradish and 2 tablespoonfuls of celery seed. Boil the seasoning in ½ gallon of vinegar and pour over the whole.

CHILI SAUCE (H.S. NORTHUP)

12 tomatoes
3 green peppers (jalapeño)
2 onions
2 tablespoons salt
2 tablespoons sugar
1 tablespoon cinnamon
3 cups vinegar

You will need 12 large ripe tomatoes, 4 ripe or 3 green peppers, 2 onions, 2 tablespoonfuls of salt, 2 of sugar, 1 of cinnamon and 3 cupfuls of vinegar. Peel tomatoes and onions and chop fine, separately; add the peppers, chopped, with other ingredients and boil for 1½ hours.

Author's note: I'm assuming the green peppers may be chili peppers, like a green cayenne or jalapeño, as bell peppers give off no heat.

SPICED PEACHES
(MRS. M.A. GORMLEY)

2 gallons peaches
2 pounds sugar
3 pints vinegar
2 ounces powdered cinnamon
2 ounces powdered cloves

You will need 1 peck of peaches pared, 2 pounds of sugar and 3 pints of vinegar. Boil the sugar and vinegar together; throw over the peaches boiling hot; let them stand for 3 days. Boil the syrup again and throw over the peaches again, then add to the syrup 2 ounces of cinnamon, 2 ounces of cloves; boil it well and throw over the peaches and tie up for use.

PICKLED OYSTERS
(MRS. R. BUSHNEL)

2 pints oysters, shucked
Equal amounts vinegar and oyster juice
Mace
Lemon peel
Powdered cloves

Place oysters in a saucepan and let them simmer in their juice for 10 minutes; place in a jar and cover. When cold, add pickle—same quantity of vinegar as juice—mace, lemon peel, cloves; boil 5 minutes. When cold, pour over oysters and tie down very close.

HOT WATER SPONGE CAKE (MRS. WENTWORTH)

6 eggs
3 cups flour
2 cups sugar
1 cup hot water
1 tablespoon yeast powder
2 cups flour
2 cups sugar
4 eggs
½ cup water
2 teaspoons baking powder

You will need 6 eggs, 3 cupfuls of flour, 2 of sugar, 1 of hot water and 1 tablespoonful of yeast powder. Place in hot water last and beat for 15 minutes. Then you will need 2 cupfuls each of flour and sugar and 4 fresh eggs. Beat the yolks and whites separately. Then add ½ cupful water and 2 teaspoonfuls baking powder and bake in a quick oven.

GINGER SNAPS (MRS. S.C. HITTE)

1 cup dark brown sugar
1 cup molasses
½ cup butter
¼ cup sour milk or buttermilk
Pinch baking soda
1 tablespoon ginger
Flour

You will need 1 cupful of brown sugar, 1 cupful of molasses, ½ cupful of butter, ¼ cupful of sour milk, a little baking soda, 1 tablespoonful of ginger and flour to make stiff enough to roll and cut up.

GRAPE CATSUP
(*20TH CENTURY COOKBOOK*, 1912)

5 pounds grapes
1 pint vinegar
3 pounds sugar
1 tablespoon cinnamon
1 teaspoon ground cloves
1 teaspoon allspice
1 teaspoon ground pepper
½ teaspoon salt

You will need 5 pounds grapes, cooked and rubbed through a sieve; 1 pint of vinegar; 3 pounds of sugar; 1 tablespoon of ground cinnamon; 1 teaspoon of cloves; 1 teaspoon of allspice; 1 teaspoon of pepper; and ½ teaspoon of salt. Boil until thick.

RECIPE FOR QUARRELING
(*20TH CENTURY COOKBOOK*, 1912)

Take a root of sassafras and steep it in a pint of water; then put in a bottle. And when your husband comes into quarrel, fill your mouth with it and hold until he goes away. A sure cure.

ROAST PIGEONS
(*20TH CENTURY COOKBOOK*, 1912)

2 pigeons
2 tablespoons flour
1 tablespoon butter

Pigeons lose their flavor when they are kept more than one day after being killed. They may be prepared, roasted and broiled the same as chicken; they will require between 20 and 30 minutes of cooking. Make a gravy using the giblets, or not; season with pepper and salt, and a little flour and butter.

MEXICAN RICE USUALLY GOOD ("THE BROSNAHAM MANUSCRIPT COOKBOOK," 1925)

½ cup dry rice
1 tablespoon butter
½ cup tomato juice
½ onion, chopped
1 cup chicken or vegetable stock
Salt and pepper to taste

Use ½ cupful rice, washed and drained well, and then fry the rice in 1 tablespoon of butter until the rice has browned nicely, stirring constantly. Add to the mixture after browning ½ cupful strained tomato juice and a little chopped onion. Cook for 2 minutes, and then add 1 cupful of thin soup stock, strained, salt and pepper. Cover and let simmer until all the water has been absorbed. The rice, when done, will be perfectly soft and retain its shape, and it will be a delicate pink color. Daddy will like this.

Mrs. Peggy Stearns (1867–1945) lived in Pensacola from the 1920s until her death in 1945. I found a newspaper clipping from May 1938 that announces an annual recital of her music pupils in the Coca-Cola Rooms. During the Great Depression, Peggy partnered with WCOA AM Radio and Piggly Wiggly grocery stores to compile a cookbook of recipes from local ladies. The purpose of this book was to show local ladies how to stretch a dollar for their families with frugal but filling recipes.

The introduction of the book reads:

> *This book of recipes has been made possible by the cooperation of WCOA and Piggly Wiggly stores with the ladies of Pensacola and vicinity who have so freely contributed their original and valued recipes, hoping that the housewives of this community will profit by their experience in preparing dainty and wholesome dishes at low cost, most of the recipes being based on economy as well as being palatable. We hope that the book will be of assistance to you in preparing a daily menu that will be well balanced and satisfactory and make possible an agreeable change of dishes from day to day.*
> *—THE PUBLISHERS*

Left and opposite: Peggy's Piggly Wiggly Recipe Book cover and recipes. *University of West Florida Archives; author's collection.*

Mrs. Stearns was affectionately known as the WCOA Piggly Wiggly Girl. The following recipes are from that cookbook.

CLOVER LEAF SALAD (BEATRICE POTTS)

2 packages cream cheese
8 stuffed olives
Mayonnaise
3 large peppers
Lettuce

Add cream cheese with chopped olives and a little mayonnaise. Pack well into pepper shells. Chill thoroughly, slice and serve on lettuce.

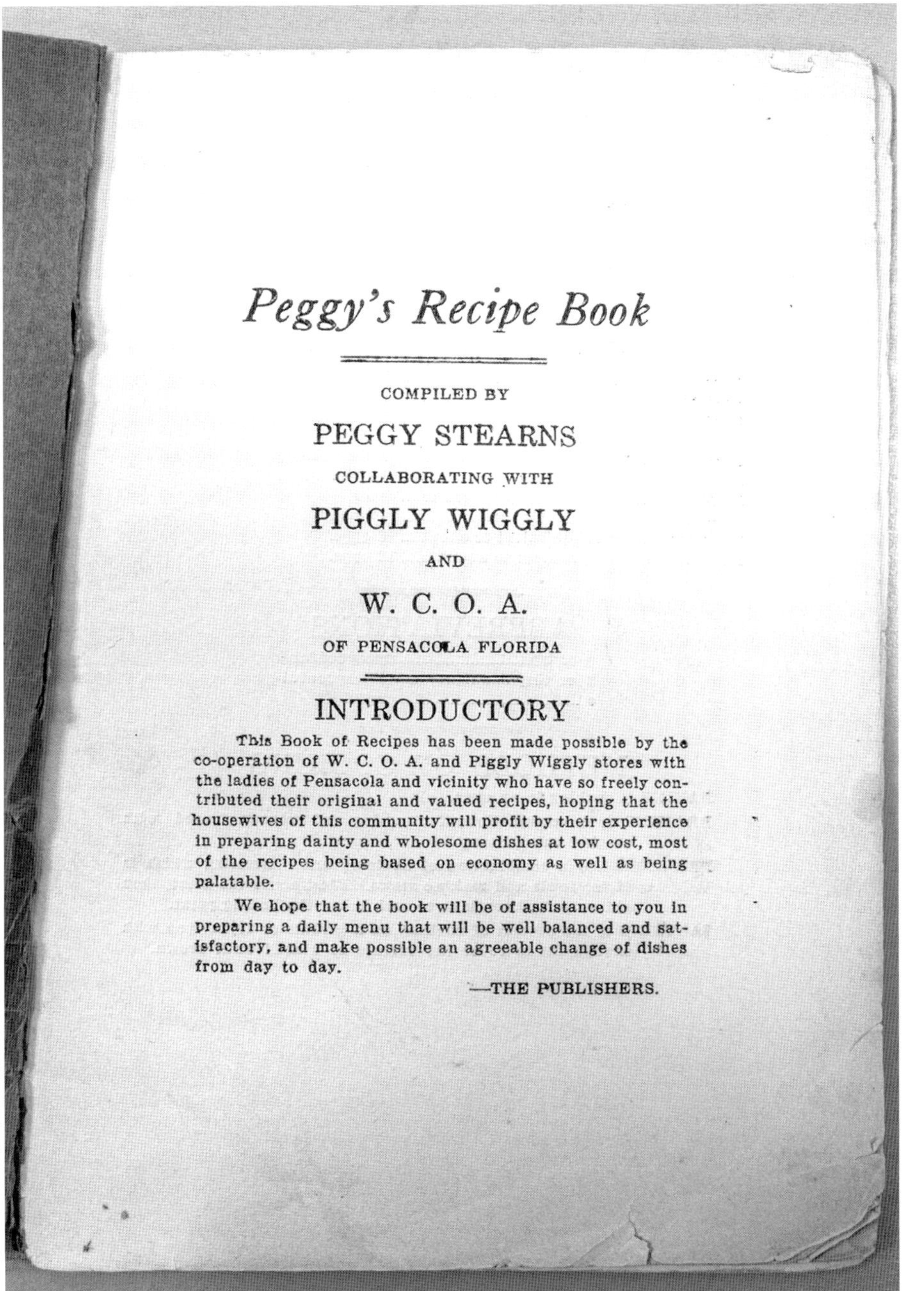

Peggy's Recipe Book

COMPILED BY

PEGGY STEARNS

COLLABORATING WITH

PIGGLY WIGGLY

AND

W. C. O. A.

OF PENSACOLA FLORIDA

INTRODUCTORY

This Book of Recipes has been made possible by the co-operation of W. C. O. A. and Piggly Wiggly stores with the ladies of Pensacola and vicinity who have so freely contributed their original and valued recipes, hoping that the housewives of this community will profit by their experience in preparing dainty and wholesome dishes at low cost, most of the recipes being based on economy as well as being palatable.

We hope that the book will be of assistance to you in preparing a daily menu that will be well balanced and satisfactory, and make possible an agreeable change of dishes from day to day.

—THE PUBLISHERS.

CONGEALED APPLE SALAD (MRS. GEORGE LEPARDE)

1 pack lime Jell-O
1 cup shredded cabbage
1 cup chopped apples
½ cup chopped olives
Lettuce
Mayonnaise

Dissolve Jell-O in 1 pint of boiling water; stir until dissolved, and place in icebox [refrigerator]. When it begins to congeal, add cabbage, apples and olives. Place in icebox until firm. Serve on lettuce leaf with mayonnaise.

FLAPPER PEGGY SALAD (MRS. C.L. KINDRED)

1 can pears, whole
Mayonnaise
Fresh lettuce leaves
Few whole cloves
Few drops red cake coloring
Small amount of pimentos
1 can shredded coconut (or same amount of shredded American cheese)

Place one half of a canned pear on a dollop of mayonnaise on a lettuce leaf so that the smaller part of the pear acts as a chin for the flapper. Place cloves for the eyes, two drops of red cake coloring for the nose and a small piece of a pimento cut in the shape of a heart for the mouth. Shredded American cheese or coconut is used for the hair. If coconut is used, it may be colored red, brown or black. If served at a luncheon, bride party, etc., a small "birthday cake" candle placed in the mouth and lit before serving makes the "flapper" even more attractive. Tiny cheese crackers arranged around the head part serve for a hat.

CARROTS À LA KING (MRS. T.J. GLADWELL)

4 cups diced carrots
1 tablespoon minced pimentos
1 tablespoon minced parsley
1 teaspoon grated onion
2 cups white sauce (bechamel)

Cook diced carrots until tender; then drain. Add vegetables to hot sauce and pour over carrots.

POTATO PONE (MRS. G.H. PAYNE)

1 quart grated sweet potatoes
⅜ cup melted butter
1 teaspoon nutmeg
½ bottle lemon extract
¼ cup sweet milk
1½ cups sugar

Mix ingredients in order given. Pour in a loaf pan and bake very slowly until brown.

OYSTER PAN ROAST (MRS. J. WARREN BATTLE)

1 tablespoon horseradish
2 tablespoons catsup
2 tablespoons Worcester sauce
½ teaspoon TABASCO® sauce
1 teaspoon prepared mustard
½ lemon
½ block butter
½ teaspoon salt
Dash pepper
1 quart oysters

Mix ingredients with oysters, place in a baking dish and bake for 30 minutes in a moderate oven. Serve with crisp fried bacon and hot buttered toast.

HAM LOAF WITH MINT PEARS (MRS. OTTO P. REAM JR.)

1 pound ground ham
¾ pound ground pork shoulder
1 egg
¼ cup milk
⅛ teaspoon pepper

Mix in order given and bake in a loaf pan for 1 hour. Garnish with mint pears.

Mint Pears

1 (14-ounce) can pears
1 package cream cheese
Mint syrup

Place pear halves cut side up in a baking dish and fill each half with cream cheese. Pour syrup in the bottom of the dish. Bake at 275 degrees. While baking, baste with the syrup. Bake for 20 minutes.

BUTTERMILK PIE (MRS. JAMES A. WARD)

1 cup sugar
2 level tablespoons flour or cornstarch
Pinch salt
½ cup butter
3 eggs (save whites of 2 for top)
1 cup buttermilk
1 teaspoon vanilla extract

Sift sugar, flour and salt together; add butter, then eggs, stirring constantly. Add buttermilk and vanilla. Cook in double boiler until thick. Fill ready cooked pie crust and cover with beaten egg whites.

PIPER CAKE (MRS. CHAS W. THOMPSON)

½ cup butter
2 eggs
1 cup syrup
1 cup milk
3 cups flour
1 teaspoon cloves, ground
½ teaspoon nutmeg
1 teaspoon baking soda

Cream butter and add eggs, syrup and milk. Sift dry ingredients; add. Bake in a shallow pan.

CORN FLAKES MACAROONS (MRS. F.B. HOWLAND)

2 egg whites
1 cup sugar
2 cups corn flakes
½ (14-ounce) can coconut

Beat egg whites stiff; add sugar, corn flakes and coconut (dry). Stir with a fork. Drop on waxed paper or a greased cookie sheet. Bake in a slow oven for about 30 minutes.

In the 1930s, The Saunders Fish Company had a dilemma. It was processing tons of fish and shipping it all over the United States, even during the Depression. There was a lot of leftover fish bits that weren't really edible. You can imagine the absolute stink all this cast-off fish meat, bones and heads were causing in the summer heat. In order to make the business profitable, the company decided to repurpose the stuff. Someone had the idea of making it into cat food. Cats love fish, right? So, they processed all the cast-off parts into cat food and canned it. Fancy labels were printed, and the cat food was shipped all over the United States. At first, the cans flew off the shelves. Gourmet cat food made from Pensacola fish was really something. The first batch sold out quickly. The Saunders family awaited new orders to come pouring in. Those orders never came. Turns out, cats hated the stuff. They wouldn't touch it. Saunders Fish Co. had three boxcars loaded to the brim with cans of cat food that no cat wanted. The experiment was a failure. Some of the Saunders family members, to this day, still think it was a good idea. Alas.

In the 1940s, things changed drastically due to World War II. Food rationing was in effect, so cooks and housewives had to get creative with what was available. My great-grandmother grew her victory garden right where my neighbor's garage now sits. Meatless meals became a necessity, and dishes called "Victory Stew" and vegetable casseroles became popular. Abundant seafood was available, although it was sometimes difficult to attain, due to the possibilities of German submarines lurking in coastal waters. And of course, we can't leave out the vilified canned meat SPAM®. That particular mystery meat was not only consumed by GIs and sailors, but it was also available in the United States. And there were many interesting ways to prepare it.

VICTORY GARDEN STEW (NATIONAL MUSEUM OF AMERICAN HISTORY)

2 tablespoons lard
1 large onion, chopped
3 carrots, chopped
1 potato, chopped
1 garlic clove, minced
1 cup peas, fresh or frozen
1 cup corn kernels, fresh or frozen
2 cups broth (chicken or vegetable)
2 tablespoons vinegar or fresh lemon juice
Salt and pepper to taste
2 tablespoons chopped parsley

Warm the lard in a large stockpot over a medium heat; add onion and cook for 2 minutes. Add carrots and potato, and cook for 4 minutes. Add garlic, peas and corn, and cook for 2 minutes. Add the broth and vinegar and cook on a low heat for about 20 minutes. Season with salt, pepper and parsley and serve.

SCALLOPED CABBAGE, SPAGHETTI AND CHEESE (*A MODERN KITCHEN GUIDE*, 1946)

1 ½ cups spaghetti, broken into small pieces
3 tablespoons flour
3 tablespoons butter or other fat
2 cups milk
1 teaspoon salt
1 pound American cheese
1 quart shredded cabbage
1 cup buttered breadcrumbs

Cook spaghetti in boiling salted water for 20 minutes and drain. Make a sauce using the flour, fat, milk and salt. Shave cheese and add to hot sauce; stir until melted. Place cabbage, spaghetti and sauce in a buttered baking dish in layers and cover the top with buttered breadcrumbs. Bake for 20 to 30 minutes in a moderate oven.

RICE À LA CREOLE (*A MODERN KITCHEN GUIDE*, 1946)

1 cup chopped canned meat
1 onion
1 cup boiled rice
1 (14-ounce) can tomatoes
2 cups fine breadcrumbs
2 tablespoons butter
Celery salt
Salt and pepper

Mix above ingredients in the order given. Bake in a greased baking dish for 30 minutes at 350 degrees.

KIDNEY BEAN CASSEROLE (*A MODERN KITCHEN GUIDE*, 1946)

1 pint kidney beans
2 pared carrots
2 peeled onions
1 cup canned tomatoes
1½ teaspoons salt
1 teaspoon black pepper
1 tablespoon sugar
2 tablespoons butter
1 cup diced leftover meat

Combine kidney beans (soaked and cooked in salted water until tender) with carrots (finely chopped) and onions (thinly sliced). Heat with tomatoes for about 10 minutes and season with salt, pepper and sugar. Place the leftover meat in the bottom of a greased casserole dish; sprinkle with salt and pepper and pour over it the combined vegetables. Dot with butter, cover and cook at 400 degrees until the vegetables are tender. Serves 6 to 8.

CREOLE SHRIMP AND RICE SKILLET

4 tablespoons butter or lard, melted and divided
1 tablespoon minced garlic
Creole seasoning to taste
1⅓ cups uncooked rice
2⅔ cups chicken broth or water
1 pound peeled jumbo shrimp
1 bunch green onions, chopped
Hot sauce to taste

Melt 2 tablespoons of fat into a large skillet over medium heat. Stir in garlic, creole seasoning and rice. Stir in broth or water, bring to a boil and then reduce to a simmer, stirring occasionally. When rice is cooked, add the remaining fat and the shrimp to the rice and stir constantly for 2 to 4 minutes, or until the shrimp is cooked. Garnish with chopped green onions and hot sauce.

GREEK BAKED FISH

Olive oil
4 filets white fish (snapper, grouper, triggerfish, redfish, flounder, etc.)
1 lemon
Greek seasoning
Pinch salt
Chopped parsley

Preheat oven to 400 degrees. On a greased pan, rub olive oil on both sides of filets. Juice lemon and pour over fish. Add a generous shake of Greek seasoning and a pinch of salt. Bake for 30 minutes. Spoon pan juices over fish and serve over rice, garnish with chopped parsley.

GREEK SEASONING

3 tablespoons dried oregano
2 tablespoons dill
2 tablespoons onion powder
2 tablespoons garlic powder
½ tablespoon salt
1 tablespoon black pepper

Mix together and store in a shaker bottle.

MOCK APPLE PIE

1 (9-inch) pie shell
2 cups water
1 cup white sugar
2 teaspoons cream of tartar
30 buttery round crackers (Ritz crackers)
½ teaspoon cinnamon
1 tablespoon lemon juice

Preheat oven to 425 degrees. In a saucepan, bring water, sugar and cream of tartar to a boil. Reduce to medium-high heat, drop in whole crackers and cook for about 5 minutes. Remove from stove and add to prepared pie shell. Sprinkle cinnamon over entire pie and add lemon juice.

Topping

1 cup buttery round crackers, crushed
½ cup brown sugar
⅓ cup butter, melted
½ teaspoon ground cinnamon

For the topping, mix the crushed crackers, brown sugar and melted butter together with the ground cinnamon and sprinkle over the pie filling. Bake in the oven for 15 minutes, reduce the heat to 350 degrees and bake for another 20 minutes. Let cool slightly and serve.

TOMATO GUMBO

1 medium onion, chopped
½ green bell pepper, diced
1 stalk celery, diced
1 teaspoon butter
3 cups diced tomatoes, fresh
1 cup corn kernels
2 cups sliced okra
Salt and pepper to taste
Creole seasoning to taste
4 cups water or broth

In a small soup pot, sauté onion, bell pepper and celery with the butter over medium heat for 10 minutes. Do not brown. Add tomatoes, corn, okra and salt, pepper and Creole seasoning if using. Occasionally stirring, let it cook while you let tomatoes release their juices. When the mixture is thickened and broken down, add water and bring to a boil. Reduce heat and let simmer at least 20 minutes. Serve over rice.

MOLASSES PIE

5 eggs
1 teaspoon flour
1 cup sugar
½ cup room-temperature butter
1 teaspoon allspice
1 teaspoon clove powder
Salt to taste
1½ cups molasses

Mix all ingredients but molasses until thoroughly blended. Bring molasses to a boil and add to the mixture. Stir well and place into 2 prepared pie crusts. Bake until firm.

OYSTERS ON A STICK (*PENSACOLA QUADRICENTENNIAL COOKBOOK*, 1959)

1 slice bacon for each oyster
1 pint oysters
Butter
Lemon juice

Cut bacon into 1-inch pieces. On a skewer, alternate 2 oysters and 1 piece of bacon until the skewer is filled. You will probably use 18 oysters per stick. Broil 2 or 3 inches from flame, turning until brown. The oysters will shrink greatly. Salting is unnecessary. To melted butter, add lemon juice to taste and serve in a pitcher so that each person may pour their own sauce over oyster stick. Serves 3.

9

TWENTIETH CENTURY, PART II

By 1960, food was beginning to become homogeneous. Refrigeration and shipping was fast and efficient. Advertising was aimed at the modern homemaker, with everything focused on how to make something quick that didn't require hours and hours of preparation and cooking in the kitchen. Canned and other prepared foods became ubiquitous, and many Americans began to lose their way concerning local cooking traditions. By 1980, the microwave oven was a common sight in many homes, and whole cookbooks were published on how to cook in one. Boy, did we miss the mark on that. TV dinners gave way to a multitude of frozen microwaveable dinners, promising reduced-calorie goodness that are really just "frankenfoods" that aren't very healthy at all. From the 1950s to the 1970s, people attempted to get creative with gelatin, which led to some truly bizarre concoctions that have, by now, probably been banned by the Geneva Convention as a danger to mankind—not to mention just a bad idea of biblical proportions. Women's magazines regularly published many recipes that were clipped and slid into recipe boxes all over the country. Grandma's recipes got handed down and continue to get handed down, and they are still made in home kitchens all over Pensacola—my own included.

Things got better. Many of our Creole and Southern traditions still hold sway in Pensacola. Abundant and affordable seafood continued to be a staple, albeit most of what was available could be found cooked three ways:

fried, broiled or grilled. When a restaurant wanted to get "fancy," a mornay sauce was slathered over the top of a snapper filet, and we thought it was quite something. We found our way out of it later on. Much of that has to do with the internet and The Food Network.

Any recipe you want can be found on the internet. Many people don't collect cookbooks anymore because whatever you want is just a click away (more's the pity). Cookbooks are available on hundreds of websites, and more and more are being published yearly. The Food Network kicked off a culinary craze. Originally, the programming was a bunch of shows featuring chefs making recipes. Then the competition shows hit, and everything changed. *Iron Chef*, originally from Japan, was the forerunner, and now, over half of the programming on the channel are competition shows. Some big celebrity chefs came from those tv shows, including Rachael Ray, Guy Fieri, Giada De Laurentiis, Bobby Flay, Tyler Florence—I could go on.

Cooking changed dramatically in the forty years between 1960 and 2000, and the following recipes in this final chapter will highlight some of the highs (and lows) of Pensacola's cuisine.

FRIED MULLET

This dish could've ended up anywhere in this book, but I decided to put it here. If there was ever a signature dish that represents Pensacola, it's fried mullet. The genus of the mullet fish can be found in waters all over the planet.

The two local species are the silver and the black mullet. Mullet is considered a trash fish almost everywhere else but here. We are frowned on for eating the fish that other places feel has a nasty taste and is only good for bait. However, it is due to the local waters that our mullet tastes good. Let me explain. Mullet are vegetarians, eating mostly algae and plant matter. They won't strike a baited hook, and it is virtually impossible to catch them with a fishing pole. Since there is a gill net ban in Florida, cast nets thrown from over the shoulder are the only way they can be caught.

Being algae eaters, they are mostly bottom feeders, so whatever they eat is found bouncing along the sea floor. Pensacola has pristine white beach sand, which is pure quartz crystal that was washed down from the Appalachian Mountains thousands of years ago. The food the mullet eat

Fried mullet, probably *the* signature dish in Pensacola. Mullet outsells other fish about three to one. *Author's collection.*

here is pure and unadulterated. Just sixty miles to the east sits Mobile, Alabama. Mississippi River mud coats the sea floor from Mobile to the west. From Tampa Bay and points south, the ocean floor is not as pure as it is here. So, it is only in this few-hundred-mile stretch where mullet actually tastes good. The fish are literally dining from an all-you-can-eat vegan organic salad bar their whole lives. Their meat is firm, white and very tasty. Everywhere else, the mullet's food is muddy, and it gets into the fish and turns their meat brown, mushy and completely inedible. Mullet is the number one top-selling fish in Pensacola. It outsells other fish about three to one. If you go to a fish fry in Pensacola, you'll be eating mullet (unless some good ol' boys went up the river and caught a mess of bream).

Pensacola folks usually consume mullet only two ways: fried or smoked. The smoked mullet usually turns up in fish dip, but fried is the main way to go. I love a good piece of beer-battered fried cod à la British fish and chips, but fish along the Gulf Coast is fried with cornmeal and sometimes cracker meal. There are some decent ready-mix fry stuff in bags, but my Southern ancestors would disturbingly haunt me if I didn't do it the traditional way.

8 mullet filets
1 quart buttermilk
Canola or peanut oil for frying
2 eggs, beaten
¾ cup flour
¾ cup fresh cornmeal
2 teaspoons salt
4 teaspoons powdered garlic
1 teaspoon powdered cayenne
Pepper to taste
2 teaspoons onion powder
Lemon slices

Marinate mullet in buttermilk overnight. When filets are ready to fry, remove and pat dry with paper towel. Heat oil to 350 degrees. Beat egg and place in a pie plate. Add flour to another pie plate. In a third pie plate, mix cornmeal with dry seasonings. Dredge filets in flour, then dip into beaten egg to coat thoroughly and dredge into cornmeal. Deep fry for about 5 minutes, or until golden brown. Drain on a plate with a paper towel to absorb the oil. Squeeze lemon juice on filets and eat.

SPAGHETTIOS® AND FRANKS JELL-O MOLD

¼ cup water
¼ cup condensed tomato soup
2 cans SpaghettiOs®
2 (¼ ounce) packets unflavored gelatin
4 hot dogs, cut in half through the middle

Combine water, tomato soup and SpaghettiOs in a large saucepan over medium-high heat. Gently stir as you mix in the gelatin. Continue stirring slowly for 5 minutes until there are no lumps of gelatin. Pour the mixture into a mold. Refrigerate for 4 to 5 hours, or more. When you're ready to serve this, use warm water to loosen the cake from the mold. If you're using a silicone mold, make sure the water is really hot. Place cut hot dogs standing on end in the middle of the cake. Good luck.

UNDER THE SEA GELATIN SALAD

1 package lime gelatin
¼ teaspoon salt
1 cup boiling water
1 can pear halves
1 tablespoon lemon juice
1 tablespoon lime juice
6 ounces cream cheese
⅛ teaspoon powdered ginger

Dissolve gelatin and salt in boiling water. Drain pears, measuring ¾ cup syrup. Dice pears and set aside. Add pear syrup and lemon and lime juice to gelatin. Measure 1¼ cups of mixture into 1-quart mold. Chill until set, but not firm. Meanwhile, soften cream cheese until smooth. Gradually add remaining gelatin mixture, blending until smooth. Add ginger and chill until very thick. Fold in pears and spoon into mold. Chill until firm and remove from mold. Serve on a bed of crisp lettuce.

I could go on with even worse recipes that I found, but I doubt you would cook them, so I'll stop here.

In 1957, the City of Pensacola partnered with local businesses (as advertisers) to produce a cookbook for newly arrived citizens titled *Welcome Stranger, Here Is Your Copy of Fine and Unusual Recipes*. The covers were made using actual wood planks, and it was sort of spiral-bound using four thick plastic rings. I was able to view a copy in the archive at the John Pace Library on the campus of University of West Florida. The following five recipes are from that cookbook.

AVOCADO PASTE

1 ripe avocado
1 clove garlic

Mash 1 ripe avocado through a strainer into a bowl that has been rubbed with garlic. Add enough mayonnaise so that the resulting mixture will be of spreading consistency. Add lime or lemon juice and salt to taste. Arrange potato chips on a large plate around a small bowl of the paste you have just made. Canned minced clams may be finely chopped and added to the mixture for an added delicacy.

CHOW MEIN

2 large onions, diced
2 cloves garlic, chopped
1 pound pork, diced
2 cups diced chicken
2 large green peppers, diced
4 carrots, diced
2 cups diced celery
1 package egg noodles
1 cup fat
Soy sauce to taste

Fry onions, garlic and meat until tender; add vegetables and steam until done. Boil noodles in water until fully cooked; drain and fry noodles in a little fat until they are dry and not sticky. Mix noodles with meat and vegetables and season with soy sauce.

SHEPPARD SHRIMP

2 medium onions, chopped
2 bell peppers, diced
2 cloves garlic, chopped
2 tablespoons olive oil
6 fresh tomatoes, quartered
2 pounds raw shrimp, peeled
½ cup sherry
Salt and pepper to taste

Sauté onions, peppers and garlic in olive oil until onions are clear. Add tomatoes and simmer for 15 minutes. Add shrimp, season to taste and simmer for 30 minutes.* Add sherry just before serving. Serve over rice.

**Author's note: For the love of all that is holy, do not add your shrimp that early in the process unless you like rubbery chew toys. This will drastically overcook the shrimp. Add them about 5 minutes before serving to keep them firm and sweet.*

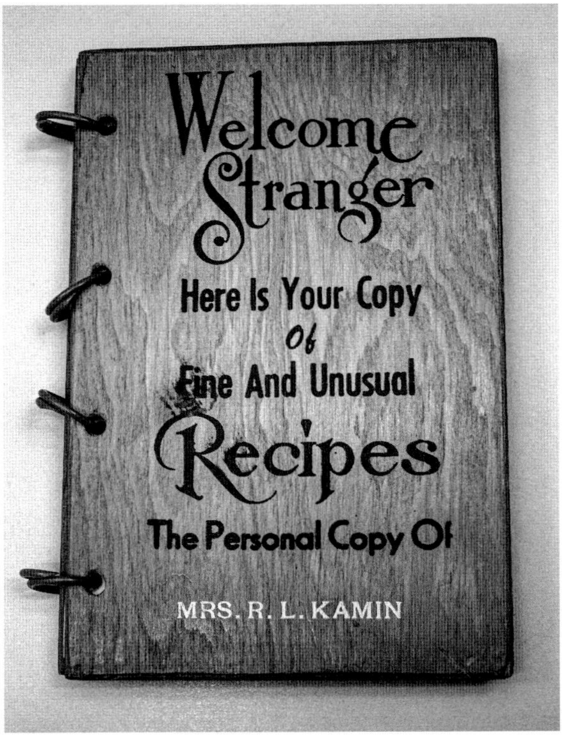

Cover and recipes from the *Welcome Stranger* cookbook. *University of West Florida Archives; author's collection.*

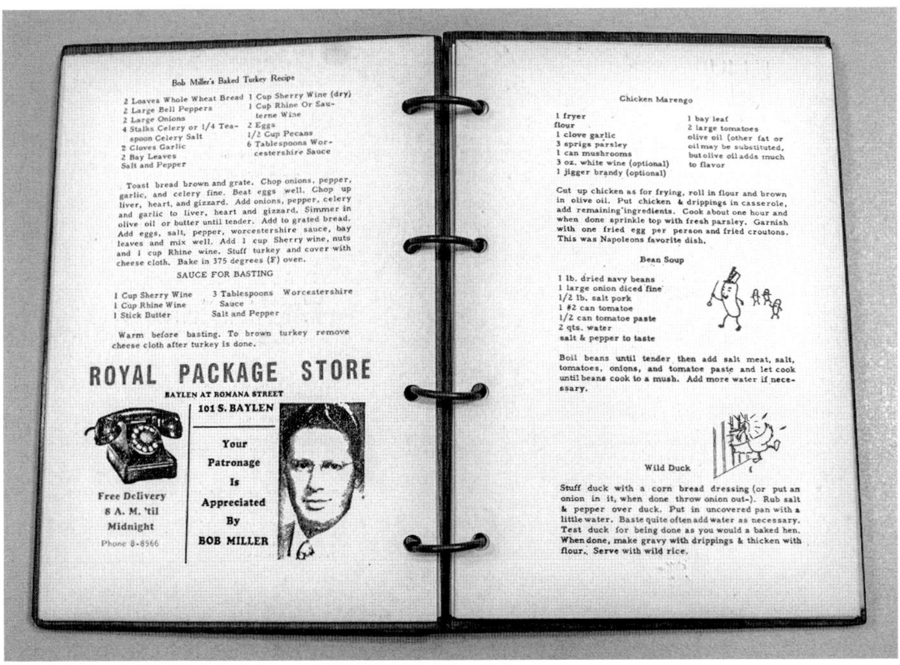

FILIPINO SWISS STEAK

1 pound round steak, cut thick
Flour
Lard or cooking fat
1 large onion, diced
2 cloves garlic, diced
2 carrots, diced
2 stalks celery, diced
1 (8-ounce) can tomato sauce
1 (8-ounce) can mushrooms
1 cup water
Salt and pepper to taste

Dust steak with flour and fry in 2 tablespoons of fat until brown. Fry onion, garlic, carrots and celery in fat until tender, and add 1 tablespoon of flour and let cook for 2 minutes. Then add tomato sauce, mushrooms and water. Salt and pepper to taste. Let meat cook in gravy for two hours. Serve with rice.

SLUM GULLION

4 slices bacon
1 medium onion
1 can tomatoes
½ pound beef, cut into small pieces
¼ pound cheese [I'm assuming cheddar], diced

Brown bacon and onions together; add tomatoes and beef and cook until meat is tender. Add cheese and cook until it is melted. Serve on bread or toast.

The Driftwood Restaurant was one of Pensacola's premier fine dining places and opened in 1976. It was located at 27 West Garden Street, directly across from the San Carlos Hotel. It was known for its seafood-forward fare as well as a vast array of fine desserts. It closed its doors in 1986. Here's some of their dishes.

BROILED SHRIMP DE JONGHE

6 tablespoons butter
¾ teaspoon minced garlic
1 pound shrimp, peeled, deveined
¼ cup sherry wine
1 tablespoon sliced green onion
½ teaspoon salt
¼ teaspoon cayenne pepper
¼ teaspoon paprika
½ cup dry plain breadcrumbs

Preheat oven to 350 degrees. Grease a 1-quart casserole dish. Melt butter in a medium-size saucepan over medium-low heat. Add garlic and sauté for 30 seconds. Stir in shrimp, sherry, green onion, salt, cayenne and paprika. Add 6 tablespoons of the breadcrumbs and stir until moistened. Transfer the mixture to the casserole dish. Sprinkle remaining breadcrumbs on top and bake for 25 minutes, or until browned and cooked through. Serve hot.

SLICED EGGS RAVIGOTE

6 tablespoons sherry wine vinegar
2 tablespoons Dijon mustard
1 cup sunflower or safflower oil
¼ cup fresh tarragon, chopped
¼ cup fresh Italian parsley, chopped
¼ cup drained capers, chopped
¼ cup shallots, chopped
¼ cup sweet gherkin pickles, chopped
6 hard-boiled eggs, peeled and sliced

Whisk vinegar and mustard in medium bowl to blend. Gradually whisk in oil. Stir in tarragon, parsley, capers, shallots and pickles. Season with salt and pepper to taste. The sauce can be made up to 2 hours ahead; let stand at room temperature. Pour over sliced hard-boiled eggs.

One thing The Driftwood was known for was their famous horseradish salad recipe. This is one of those gelatin recipes that sounds weird but is actually quite good.

DRIFTWOOD HORSERADISH SALAD

2 boxes gelatin (one lemon, one lime)
1 cup hot water
1 (14-ounce) can crushed pineapple, undrained
3 tablespoons horseradish
1 cup mayonnaise
1 cup cottage cheese
1 cup Cool Whip or sour cream
½ cup chopped pecans or walnuts
3 tablespoons chopped pimentos
3 tablespoons chopped red cherries

Dissolve gelatin in hot water; add the crushed pineapple (undrained). Allow gelatin to set but not thicken fully. Mix the rest of the ingredients together and fold into the gelatin. Allow to chill until firm. Serve with sweet whipped cream or sour cream.

BLACKENED REDFISH

This dish became famous in the 1980s thanks to celebrity chef Paul Prudhomme. The technique dates back farther, however. Redfish, or the red drum, is a wonderfully delicious fish that is abundant in the shallow waters of the Gulf of Mexico and bays and bayous along the Gulf Coast. Its wasn't a popular fish to eat outside of those areas. The blackening technique was believed to have originated in the 1800s in the French Quarter of New Orleans. Before blackening, the fish was prepared by baking or frying it. Blackening is a technique that sears meat on a very hot, dry cast iron skillet. In the 1980s, Paul Prudhomme put his own spin on the dish. He created his own seasoning blend called "Blackened Redfish Magic," and he made a fortune selling bottles of the stuff. In

Chef Prudhomme's version, the fish is dipped in melted butter, generously coated in the blackening seasoning, and placed on the skillet. It takes only a couple of minutes per side to cook the dish.

This dish had some very unfortunate consequences. It became immensely popular, and demand for redfish soared so much that they quickly became overfished, and the very existence of the species was threatened. Today, there are very strict regulations regarding the size and number of your catch of redfish. Legal fish are called "slot reds," because they need to be in between certain lengths, which vary year to year. Usually, they fall somewhere between eighteen to twenty-eight inches, Redfish can get *big*. I caught a thirty-six-inch redfish before. And they fight like a drunken sailor, so they're very fun to catch. In the state of Florida, anglers are allowed only one slot red per person per day.

4 to 6 redfish filets or any other firm white fish (Grouper tends to be too thick for blackening, but snappers, triggerfish and flounder work well.)
¼ stick (2 tablespoons) melted unsalted butter
Blackened redfish seasoning

Heat a dry cast iron skillet or other large skillet on a high heat for at least 6 to 7 minutes. Dredge the filets in butter, coating both sides well. Add a generous coating of the seasoning to both sides of the filet and place into the pan. Cook each side for about 1½ to 2 minutes. Remove and serve. Beware, this technique produces a lot of smoke, so do this in a well-ventilated area.

BLACKENED REDFISH SEASONING

1 tablespoon sweet or smoked paprika
2½ teaspoons salt
1 teaspoon onion powder
1½ teaspoons garlic powder
1 teaspoon cayenne powder
1 teaspoon white pepper
½ teaspoon black pepper
¾ teaspoon dried thyme

Mix ingredients well. This seasoning works on all kinds of meat and vegetables; it's not just for blackening.

The Yacht was a small ship that served as a floating restaurant located in Pitt's Slip in downtown Pensacola. Formerly called *The Good Neighbor*, the boat had an amazing past, serving as a dignitary vessel, a dive boat in South America and even a depth charge boat in World War II. From 1986 to 1999, it was a unique place where Pensacola folks dined. The following is a popular recipe from that restaurant.

CHARGRILLED GROUPER WITH RED BELL PEPPER SAUCE

Fish

2 filets grouper
Olive oil
Salt and pepper to taste

Sauce

1 (16-ounce) jar roasted red peppers
4 cloves garlic
2 tablespoons butter
½ teaspoon dried basil
Black pepper to taste
½ cup heavy cream
Salt and pepper to taste

Rub filet with oil and salt and pepper. Grill or broil for up to 8 minutes per side, depending on thickness. Make sure the fish is cooked through without being overdone.

Place red peppers in a blender, along with about 2 tablespoons of the liquid from the jar. Purée the peppers until smooth, adding 1 or 2 tablespoons of water if needed to help it blend.

Mince the garlic and add it to a skillet with the butter. Sauté the garlic in the butter over medium-low heat for 1 to 2 minutes, or just until the garlic has softened, do not brown. Pour in the puréed peppers and add the dried basil and some freshly cracked pepper. Mix well with a spoon. Bring sauce to a simmer. Set heat to low and let the sauce simmer for 10 to 15 minutes, or until the mixture is thickened, stirring often.

Add cream to the skillet; stir until the sauce is smooth, and allow it to heat through. Add salt and pepper to taste and serve over fish.

PASTITSIO (GREEK LASAGNA)

Base Ingredients

15 ounces bucatini pasta, penne or ziti
2 egg whites
4 ounces feta cheese

Meat Sauce

30 ounces lean ground beef
2 medium red onions, chopped
2 cloves garlic, chopped
14 ounces canned diced tomatoes
1 tablespoon tomato paste
1 teaspoon sugar
5 fluid ounces red wine
3 bay leaves
1 cinnamon stick
1 whole clove
¼ cup olive oil
Salt and pepper to taste

Bechamel Sauce

4.3 ounces butter
4.3 ounces plain flour
34 ounces milk
2 egg yolks
Salt and pepper to taste
1 pinch nutmeg
1.7 ounces Kefalotyri or Parmigiano-Reggiano
Additional Kefalotyri or Parmigiano-Reggiano to sprinkle

Preheat oven to 350 degrees. To prepare bechamel, melt butter in a large pan over low-medium heat. Add the flour, whisking continuously to make a paste. Add warmed milk in small batches, whisking briskly to prevent lumps. Remove the pan from the stove and add egg yolks, salt, pepper, a pinch of nutmeg and grated cheese. Whisk very quickly to prevent eggs from becoming a frittata. Add salt as needed.

For the meat sauce, brown ground beef in a skillet, remove and drain. On medium high heat, sauté onions and garlic until translucent (about 8 minutes), add the rest of the ingredients and simmer on medium low heat for 1 hour, stirring occasionally.

Cook the pasta until it is al dente. Drain and stir in egg whites and crumbled feta cheese; mix with a spatula. Do not over mix.

Butter the bottom and sides of large baking dish and assemble the pastitsio. Layer pasta, top with meat sauce and even out. Top meat with bechamel sauce and smooth out with a spatula. Sprinkle dish with grated cheese and bake at 350 degrees for about 40 minutes, or until crust turns a light golden brown. Let cool before serving.

PASTA MARE

¼ cup olive oil
1 to 2 cloves garlic, minced
12 grape or cherry tomatoes, cut in half
2 to 4 tablespoons parsley, chopped
1 to 2 dashes hot pepper flakes
Pinch salt
1 pound seafood of choice (shrimp, clams, firm white fish)
3 cups cooked spaghetti or linguini
Shaved Parmesan

Pasta mare. *Author's collection.*

In a large pan, add the olive oil, garlic, halved tomatoes and chopped parsley. Cook while stirring the tomatoes often for 10 minutes over medium heat. Once the tomatoes have started to blister, smash them with your wooden spoon and add the hot pepper flakes, salt and seafood. Cook covered for about 4 minutes; then uncover, raise the heat to medium-high and continue to cook for about 1 to 2 minutes, or until the sauce thickens, tossing often. Make sure it doesn't burn. Add the cooked pasta and ¼ cup pasta water, and cook on high, tossing for about 1 minute. If the pasta is too dry, add a bit more pasta water; it should be thick, almost creamy. Serve hot with a sprinkle of shaved Parmesan.

GRASSHOPPER PIE

24 OREO cookies, crushed very fine
2 tablespoons melted butter
1 large jar marshmallow fluff
¼ cup crème de menthe
1 pint heavy cream, whipped

Set aside ½ cup crushed OREOs. Mix butter into remaining cookie crumbs and press into a 9 x 9 glass baking dish. Combine marshmallow fluff and crème de menthe. Fold whipped cream into mixture. When well blended, pour into crumb crust and add remaining crumbs. Freeze until it is firm.

BAKED CHICKEN GRECIAN STYLE (ZOE STAMETELOS)

1 chicken
4 tablespoons seasoning mix (equal parts salt, paprika and oregano)
2 lemons
1 stick butter
1 or 2 potatoes, sliced

Cut chicken in serving pieces and place in baking pan, skin side down. Sprinkle with salt, paprika, oregano, and the juice from 2 lemons. Dot with 1 stick of butter and add 1 cup of water. Bake in oven, uncovered at 350F for 30 to 40 minutes. Then turn chicken and continue to bake for another 30 minutes more. Sliced potatoes may be added after the chicken has been removed from the pan. Season potatoes with salt and paprika and add more water. Bake until done, about 30 minutes, uncovered.

FRANK'S FISH CHOWDER

Frank Reed was a retired cook from the SS Tarpon. *The tarpon was a 360-foot twin screw steam packet cargo ship that operated between Mobile and Panama City from 1902 to 1907. Frank made this chowder for not only the crew but also friends all along the Gulf Coast.*

1½ cups flour
1 cup bacon grease
8 cups hot water
2 onions, chopped
1 green pepper, chopped
2 stalks celery, chopped
½ lemon, sliced
2 pods garlic, chopped
½ cup ketchup with 1½ tablespoon allpice added
1 (6-ounce) can tomato paste
4 medium potatoes, cubed
4 pound fish pieces

Brown flour in the bacon grease; stir in the hot water. Add the other ingredients, except the potatoes and fish. Cook for 1 hour and 15 minutes. Add cubed potatoes and cook for 15 minutes; then add the fish and cook for 5 minutes.

SHRIMP AND GRITS

Lord above! This dish is definitely one of the most popular in Pensacola. Its origins begin in Charleston, South Carolina, in 1950 as a breakfast item in the *Charleston Receipts Cookbook*. By 1976, it was so popular that it became the official state food of South Carolina. Shrimp and grits is on the menu in many Pensacola restaurants, but it is arguably The Fish House's "Grits a' Ya Ya" that kicked off the craze. The following is a variation of their famous and most popular dish.

Grits

¾ cup old-fashioned grits
3½ cups chicken stock
¼ cup heavy cream, add more as needed
1 cup smoked Gouda cheese, shredded (or more to taste)
¼ cup butter

Shrimp Sauce

3 tablespoons minced shallot
2 tablespoons minced garlic
1 splash white wine
3 tablespoons butter
1 pound shrimp, peeled and deveined
2 cups spinach
¼ cup chopped green onions
2 cups heavy cream
Hot sauce, salt and pepper to taste

Add grits to chicken stock over high heat while stirring constantly. Reduce heat to low; simmer until grits thicken, 15 to 20 minutes, stirring occasionally. Stir in heavy cream. Stir in Gouda cheese and butter until melted and smooth.

For the shrimp sauce, heat a deep skillet over medium-high heat, cook bacon until fat is rendered, about 3 minutes. Reduce heat to medium, and stir in shallots and garlic, constantly stirring until shallots are translucent. Pour in white wine and stir in butter, cooking and stirring until butter is melted. Add shrimp and stir for 3 minutes. Stir in spinach and green onions; cook and stir until the spinach wilts, about 2 minutes. Remove shrimp with a slotted spoon. Stir in heavy cream. Simmer until the cream is reduced by about ⅓, about 10 minutes. Return shrimp to the skillet to heat through. Serve shrimp with sauce over the prepared grits. Add hot sauce, salt and pepper to taste.

GROUPER PICCATA

One of the most iconic restaurants on Pensacola Beach is The Grand Marlin, a semi–fine dining establishment directly on Quietwater Beach that offers up the most picturesque views of Santa Rosa Sound alongside upscale seafood cuisine. One of the staples on the menu is the grouper piccata. The following is a recipe that is nearly identical to theirs.

4 (6-ounce) grouper or snapper fillets
¼ teaspoon salt
¼ teaspoon pepper
¼ cup all-purpose flour

Grouper piccata, a very popular dish at The Grand Marlin Restaurant on Pensacola Beach. *Author's collection.*

3 tablespoons butter, divided
1 tablespoon olive oil
½ cup fresh lemon juice
¼ cup white wine
2 tablespoons capers
2 tablespoons chopped parsley

Sprinkle grouper fillets with salt and pepper. Dredge fillets on all sides in flour. Melt 2 tablespoons of butter and olive oil in a large skillet. Add fillets to skillet; cook until browned and cooked through, about 5 minutes on each side. Remove fish from skillet.

Add lemon juice and wine to skillet, scraping browned bits from the pan. Cook for 2 minutes, or until slightly thickened. Remove from heat; stir in remaining 1 tablespoon butter, capers and parsley. Serve sauce over fish.

What kind of cookbook author would I be if I didn't include some of my own family's recipes here? The last few recipes were some simple family favorites that we enjoyed growing up, either as a quick weeknight dinner or for family holiday traditions.

IRENE'S BEEF STROGANOFF

Irene was my mother. She made this beef stroganoff many times and passed the recipe on to me. I believe she may have clipped it out of a women's magazine at some point in the 1970s. It's a tasty recipe that is easily scaled up to feed a bunch of people.

1 pound ground beef
1 clove garlic, crushed
1 onion, sliced
1 (12-ounce) can cream of mushroom soup
1 cup sour cream
2 teaspoons Worcestershire sauce
2 tablespoons tomato ketchup
Prepared egg noodles

Brown meat in a hot skillet and drain. Add garlic and onion; cook for 5 minutes. Combine the rest of the ingredients, mix well and heat through. Serve on hot buttered egg noodles.

CHEESE PEPPER PIE

I believe it was my cousin Mary Caughman Henriques who brought this recipe home from her days as a student at the University of Florida. Nevertheless, this is always on the menu at every family gathering.

2 small cans whole green chili peppers
2 cups cheddar cheese
2 cups Swiss cheese
2 eggs
Hot sauce to taste

Preheat oven to 350 degrees. Open cans of chilis; remove (save the liquid) and cut open chilis so they may lay flat. Line the bottom of 2 pie plates with chilis so they're fully covered. Mix the cheeses together and add to the pie plates. Beat 2 eggs in the chili liquid until smooth, and add hot sauce to taste. Add equal amounts of the egg mixture to the top of each pie plate; make sure it is all around the pie. Bake for 10 minutes. Let cool, slice and eat.

ACORN SQUASH STUFFED WITH ZA'ATAR SPICED BEEF AND HARISSA YOGURT

This book wouldn't be complete without at least one of my own recipes. This was a total fluke on my part. I needed to make dinner, and this is what I had on hand. So, I created this dish on the spot one evening, and now it's a staple in our home on cold winter evenings. This is my own spin on Middle Eastern cuisine.

2 acorn squashes
1 pound ground beef
Za'atar seasoning
Salt to taste
Olive oil
Unflavored full-fat Greek yogurt
Harissa seasoning

Preheat oven to 350 degrees. Slice a small section off the bottoms of the squashes so they may sit upright in a baking dish. Cut the top off of the squashes and dig out the seeds and mushy, stringy parts. In a high-heat skillet, brown the ground beef and drain. Add at least 1 teaspoon of za'atar (or more if you like) and salt to taste. Brush the squash with olive oil, inside and out. Fill the squash with the beef and place in a greased baking dish or tray. Then place in oven and bake for 30 to 40 minutes. Remove to let cool for 5 minutes. Add a generous dollop of Greek yogurt on top of the beef, and sprinkle harissa over the yogurt. Serve hot.

AFTERWORD

Thank you for reading this book. I hope you enjoyed looking into the culinary past of America's oldest settlement. Many months of research went into finding the recipes that were used in this area, dating to the first Native settlers two thousand years ago. The recipes contained in this book can all be made in the modern kitchen, and I hope you have fun trying them out. Good luck with the SpaghettiOs and Franks gelatin mold. I'm not sure I'm brave enough to try that one, but I just might.

The earlier recipes are not hard to make, but they may be considered bland for our modern palates. The recipes were interpreted as is so that you may experience what our forebears ate during their lifetimes in Pensacola. Please feel free to add any seasonings you wish to the older recipes to make them more flavorful. You just might decide to make them regular dishes in your home.

There were so many recipes that I omitted—hundreds in fact—that I wish I could have added, but I chose those that I feel best represented the cooking culture of the time. I also included some of the weirder ones because why not?

Pensacola's cuisine in the twenty-first century is now a diverse mélange that contains influences from all over the planet, a true melting pot.

Eat well!

—Duel

RECIPE NOTES

RECIPE NOTES

SELECTED BIBLIOGRAPHY

Print

Bolton, Herbert E. *The Spanish Borderlands: A Chronicle of Old Florida and the Southwest*. Yale University Press, 1921.

Bower, Ann L., ed. *African American Foodways: Explorations of History & Culture*. University of Illinois, 2009.

Gutierrez, C. Paige. *Cajun Foodways*. University Press of Mississippi, 2012.

Harris, Joy Sheffield. *A Culinary History of Florida: Prickly Pears, Datil Peppers & Key Limes*. The History Press, 2014.

Ladies of St. Francis Street Methodist Episcopal Church. *Gulf City Cookbook*. St. Francis Street Methodist Episcopal Church, 1882.

Markham, Gervase, and Michael R. Best. *The English Housewife Cookbook*. McGill-Queen's University Press, 1994.

Martinelli, Candida, ed. *The Anonymous Andalusian Cookbook*. CreateSpace, 2012.

Parker, Catherine. "Foodways and Faunal Remains at Presidio Santa Maria de Galve, 1698–1719: Between the Devil and the Deep Blue Sea." Graduate thesis, University of West Florida, 2001.

The Picayune's Creole Cookbook. New Orleans Times Picayune, 1901.

Root, Waverly, and Richard de Rochemont. *Eating in America*. HarperCollins, 1981.

Stearns, Peggy. *Peggy's Recipe Book*. Piggly Wiggly and WCOA AM Radio, circa 1935.

Welcome Stranger, Fine and Unusual Recipes. City of Pensacola, circa the 1950s.
West Florida Cookbooks. John C. Pace Library, 1983.
Zahendra, Peter. "Spanish Florida." PhD diss., University of West Florida, 1976.

Websites

Medieval and Renaissance Food: Sources, Recipes, and Articles. "The Forme of Cury." http://www.pbm.com/~lindahl/foc/.
Medieval Cookery. www.medievalcookery.com.
Mendel, Janet. *My Kitchen in Spain.* www.mykitcheninspain.blogspot.com.
Sodipe's Creations. www.sodipescreations.wordpress.com.
Stockdale, Mabel K., and Sally E. Bryenton. "Indian Plant Foods of the Florida Panhandle." February 1978. http://palmm.digital.flvc.org/islandora/object/uf%3A32648/datastream/OBJ/view/Indian_Plant_Foods_of_the_Florida_Panhandle_by_Mabel_K__Stockdale_and_Sally_E__Bryenton.pdf.

ABOUT THE AUTHOR

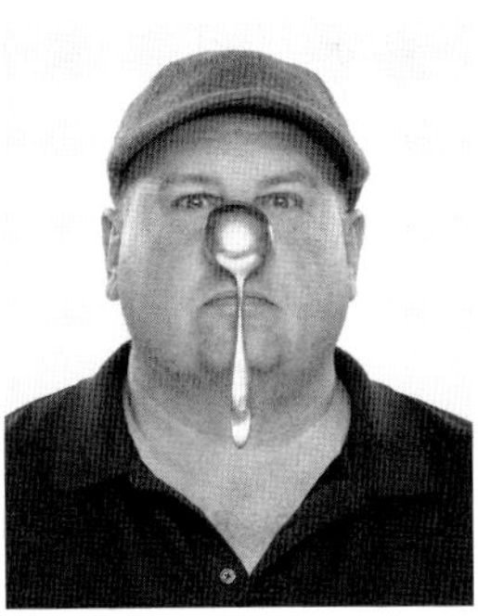

The author, Duel, being himself. *Edward McGrath.*

I am a Pensacola native, born in 1968 and baptized at First United Methodist Church, where I am still a member. I grew up immersed in Pensacola history. My grandmother Mary Wesley was a local historian, a member and past president of The Pensacola Historical Preservation Society. I was "volun-told" to attend numerous historical events growing up, including the archaeology excavations at Fort George. I ran and played at Forts Pickens and Barrancas as a child and know every inch of both places. This fostered my great love of history at a young age that continues to this day.

I was going to become an archaeologist, but life chose a different path. I got my first job in television at WSRE TV 23 PBS while attending Pensacola Junior College and never looked back. I attended Florida State University and received a degree in film and television production and spent the next twenty-eight years in television and video production. During that time, I worked on a few hundred episodes of cooking shows, both local and nationally syndicated. I worked with and met some very famous chefs during that time. I learned how to cook on a TV set. I decided to marry my love of food and history together and created Seville Savories Food Tour, a walking historical food tour in downtown Pensacola, Florida. Guests stroll through historical downtown Pensacola and dine in multiple specially selected tasting destinations to sample unique and diverse foods that were curated by me and the chefs. You can find me at www.sevillesavoriesfoodtour.com.

When I'm not guiding tours or writing, I spend most of my time with my family. I do fish when I get a chance and am a voracious reader. I also am a professional musician and was on the Celtic music circuit in the southeastern United States for many years, performing at Celtic festivals and in pubs.

Pensacola Flavor: A Culinary History with Recipes is my first book. I am currently working on other books about Pensacola's history, so stay tuned.